Civil War Ends

Assassination, Reconstruction, and the Aftermath

Civil War Ends

Assassination, Reconstruction, and the Aftermath

Corinne J. Naden & Rose Blue

RSVP

RAINTREE STECK-VAUGHN
PUBLISHERS
A Steck-Vaughn Company

Austin, Texas

www.steck-vaughn.com

For Maire Plunkett Baldwin, my favorite college kid, with love, from Corinne
For my very good friend Sam Roth, with love, from Rose

Published by Raintree Steck-Vaughn Publishers,
an imprint of Steck-Vaughn Company

Publishing Director: Walter Kossmann
Editor: Shirley Shalit
Project Management & Design: Gino Coverty
Cover Design: Gino Coverty
Media Researcher: Claudette Landry
Electronic Production: Gino Coverty
Consultant: Paul Finkelman, University of Tulsa, College of Law

Library of Congress Cataloging-in-Publication Data

Naden, Corinne J.
    Civil War ends: assassination, reconstruction, and the aftermath
/ Corinne J. Naden & Rose Blue.
        p.   cm. — (The house divided)
    Includes bibliographical references (p.   ) and index.
    Summary: Describes the aftermath of the Civil War, including the assassination of Lincoln, Reconstruction, and the presidency of Ulysses S. Grant.
    ISBN 0-8172-5583-4
    1. United States — History — 1865–1898 — Juvenile literature 2. United States — Politics and government — 1865–1900 Juvenile literature. 3. United States — History — Civil War, 1861–1865 — Influence Juvenile literature. 4. Lincoln, Abraham, 1809–1865 — Assassination Juvenile literature. 5. Slaves — Emancipation — United States Juvenile literature. 6. Reconstruction Juvenile literature. [1. Reconstruction. 2. United States — History — 1865-1898.]
    I. Blue, Rose. II. Title. III. Series: Naden, Corinne J. House divided.
    E661.N34   1999
    973.8 — dc21
                                                                99–15598
                                                                CIP   AC

Printed and bound in the United States of America
1 2 3 4 5 6 7 8 9 0 IP 03 02 01 00 99

Cover photo: Hiram Revels, first African American senator, takes the oath of office in 1870.

Title page photo: After the Civil War many cities throughout the South resembled this photo of Charleston in 1865.

Acknowledgments listed on page 112 constitute part of this page.

Contents

WILL THE HOUSE STILL STAND?

Prologue

The American Civil War began on April 12, 1861, when the newly formed Confederate States of America attacked Fort Sumter in Charleston, South Carolina. Now, four, long, bloody years later, it has ended. It is April 9, 1865. General Robert E. Lee, Army of Northern Virginia, surrenders to General Ulysses S. Grant, Army of the Potomac, at Appomattox Court House, Virginia. Small-scale fighting will continue for several weeks, and the war will not be declared officially over until May. But for most people, Appomattox is the end. The worst conflict ever fought on American soil is over.

From the North's point of view, the war was fought to preserve the Union. And so it does, but at a staggering cost.

Battle statistics are probably never 100 percent accurate. This is certainly true of the Civil War. Historians still argue about the casualty numbers. However, most sources estimate that well over 600,000 Americans died in the Civil War, about

The U.S. Capitol in Washington, D.C., at the time of Lincoln's second inauguration, March 1865. The building stands now as a symbol of a united nation.

360,000 for the North and about 258,000 for the South. That includes those who died of disease and other causes as well as in battle. Add to that the surviving wounded, some 280,000 for the North, perhaps half that for the South. Actually, soldiers on either side were more likely to die of disease than being shot on the battlefield. There are other casualties, too. Many will return home without a scratch but with the horrors of war so burned in their memory that life will never be the same again.

Now, as the war ends, the survivors think of going home. But what will they go home to?

The Yankees return to states fairly bursting with growth. Industry is booming in the North. So is the population. A soldier away from Chicago for four years simply will not recognize his own city. The population has nearly doubled. A Yank who left Washington, D.C., in 1861 said goodbye to a small, rather undignified town of about 63,000 people. The streets ran muddy in the rain and cattle grazed near the unfinished Capitol. Four years later, the cattle are gone and building is again underway. The streets, however, still run muddy in the rain.

It is not only returning soldiers who will increase the population. Immigrants are

LEADERS AGAINST WAR

U.S. General William Tecumseh Sherman wrote in his memoirs (1875): "War is cruelty, and you cannot refine it." He was referring, of course, to the Civil War in which he played a major role. But people have been speaking of or writing about war since time began. Roman statesman Cicero declared (in 52 B.C.) that "Laws are silent in time of war." Colonial statesman Benjamin Franklin thought that "There never was a good war or a bad peace." President Franklin D. Roosevelt had a simple, direct message in 1936. He said, "I have seen children starving. I have seen the agony of mothers and wives. I hate war." In the mid-twentieth century, President John F. Kennedy bluntly told the United Nations that "Mankind must put an end to war or war will put an end to mankind."

pouring in, now about 250,000 a year from Great Britain, from Germany, from Ireland, and from the Scandinavian countries of Norway, Sweden, and Denmark. They will swell some Northern cities to the bursting point. All looking for a new life, what most of them will find are overcrowded, dangerous, unhealthy slums. Sometimes packed eight or more to a room, with a bath down the hall if they are lucky, they will live in conditions that invite disease and illness. During August of 1864, for instance, some 1,700 babies died of typhoid fever in New York City alone.

But nothing—not smoke-belching factories nor overcrowding nor disease nor unruly boomtowns—can compete with the greeting that awaits Johnny Reb. For many lads in gray, the first

One water pump serves the needs of this crowded tenement in New York City's Lower East Side in 1866.

sight of their homes will be more of a shock than the first sound of cannon fire had been. A good deal of their beloved southland is in ruins. The Confederates fought for a way of life; after Appomattox, many will return to find ruin and devastation. Large areas of Richmond, Virginia; Atlanta, Georgia; Charleston and Columbia, South Carolina, are destroyed. The Shenandoah Valley is scarred and wasted. So is the valley of the Tennessee River. Plantation fields, once tended by slaves, lay burned or unplanted. In some areas, there is desolation as far as the eye can see—houses destroyed or looted, heaps of rubble and ashes, bones of dead animals in the fields, railroads that no longer run, banks closed, factories shut down. Homeless people in every town greet the ragged, starving remains of Lee's army coming home, but not in pride and triumph. Lawless bands roam the byways. They loot and terrorize. Southern hatred for the Northern victors is just beginning.

Ruined cities greeted returning Confederate soldiers. Shown here is a section of Charleston, South Carolina, in 1865.

9

Add to this the plight of hundreds of thousands of former slaves. A major issue of the Civil War was their freedom. But what happens now? Although many have farming skills, they are otherwise uneducated and untrained, without experience or means to care for themselves. How will they live? What will they do? What will the government do for them?

It is April 9, 1865. Unofficially, the American Civil War is over, the nation reunited. Slavery is gone. Yet, there remains so much loss, so much bitterness, so much hatred. Worried leaders on both sides begin to wonder if it will ever end and how to stop it.

But before the wounds can even start to heal, this reunited nation must suffer one more great, dividing blow. It is very nearly the last straw in this fragile, tottering house of blue and gray.

Will the house still stand?

A PRESIDENT DIES

1

One might have thought that General Grant's mind was not on his work that quiet afternoon of April 9, 1865, when General Lee surrendered. Grant became so involved in their conversation that Lee had to remind him gently of the purpose of the meeting. Then, some hours passed before Grant remembered to inform President Lincoln. But once the message of surrender was received, the news traveled quickly. By the next day, thousands were celebrating in the streets of Chicago and New York City. Happy people roamed the nation's capital. Lincoln even requested one of the parading bands to play "Dixie," which he said was one of the "best tunes" he'd ever heard. The following evening, he spoke to a cheering crowd from a window of the White House. Those who expected a rousing victory speech from the President were disappointed.

A great two-day victory parade, "The Grand Review," took place in Washington, D.C., on May 23-24, 1865, with onlookers enthusiastic although still saddened by Lincoln's recent death.

Instead, Lincoln spoke calmly of the "great difficulty" that lay ahead. He said that plans for Reconstruction must remain flexible, adding that he hoped black people would be given the right to vote. His message was one of no revenge. Perhaps more than any American, the President understood that harsh peace terms could only stir up more hatred.

Time and again through the long agony of war, Abraham Lincoln had shown his wisdom and compassion. Perhaps this was never more so than in his plans for the aftermath of war.

A HERO GOES HOME

After Robert E. Lee surrendered to Grant on April 9, 1865, he retired to his beloved Virginia. In poor health from the mental and physical strains of the war, he was without income at the age of 58. The U.S. government had taken over his wife's plantation in Arlington and Lee was concerned about the welfare of his seven children. He accepted the position of president of Washington College in Lexington, where he died in 1870. The school was renamed Washington and Lee University in his honor.

Robert E. Lee at home after the surrender.

Where others might call for revenge, for bringing the losers to their knees, the President had no such desire. He wanted, in his own words, "a righteous and speedy peace." Lincoln wanted to pursue a policy of "amnesty and reconciliation," which he had expressed even before the end of the war (see pages 28–29).

His was a daunting task, and Lincoln well knew it. Not only were there the social and psychological problems of bitterness and hatred to contend with. There were some very practical and urgent day-to-day living problems as well. The economy of the South was in ruins. Lincoln wanted people back at work on the farms and in the shops as soon as possible. And what of the former slaves? They may indeed be "free at last," but how could that liberty be protected, how could they best be taken into the fabric of American society?

Lincoln's policies of moderation were opposed by part of his own party, the Radical Republicans. They wanted severe changes in the South and had little sympathy for taking it easy on those

This ruined ironworks factory in Richmond, Virginia, indicates the huge rebuilding that was required for the South to return to a functioning economy.

Andrew Johnson

they considered to be traitors to the country. In general, however, the North tended to agree with the President. The war had settled the questions of secession and slavery. Now, let the country be reunited and continue, as Lincoln said at his second inauguration, "...with malice toward none, with charity toward all...."

It is just possible that with many in the North in a mood for concession and with the moderate policies of a compassionate President, the awesome postwar problems might have been solved. Lincoln believed that mutual good will and understanding could reconnect the broken halves of the divided nation. Alas, it was not to be.

On the evening of April 14, 1865, the sixteenth President of the United States was shot by an assassin. He died on the morning of April 15, just six days after the surrender at Appomattox Court House. The assassin was John Wilkes Booth, an admirer of the Confederacy, an advocate of slavery, a hater of Lincoln.

Abraham Lincoln was the first American president to be assassinated. Unfortunately, he would not be the last: James Garfield (1881), William McKinley (1901), and John F. Kennedy (1963) also died by an assassin's bullet.

Lincoln's death profoundly changed the aftermath of the American Civil War. If there was even the beginning of Northern charity toward the South, it instantly vanished, replaced by a strong desire for revenge. George Templeton Strong, a well-known lawyer in New York City, echoed the feelings of many Northerners when he said, "Let us deal with the rebels as they deserve." In the South, any feeling of hopefulness gave way to ones of fear and apprehension. Without Lincoln's firm and shrewd leadership, the Radical Republicans now had a free hand in Congress to deal with the South as they wished. And, finally, now in the White House sat Andrew Johnson. He might intend to carry out Lincoln's policies, but Johnson came nowhere near Lincoln in political know-how. And whereas he was not particularly interested in protecting the rights of the former slaves, he also resented the ex-slaveholders and wanted to punish them.

Any hope for a "righteous peace," any faint expectation of justice and healing, any optimism about a reunited house went out the window when Lincoln was shot. The nation is still dealing with the effects of that tragic night.

Mary Todd Lincoln

Strangely, it is said that the President had a sort of "warning" about his assassination. A few days before his death, he spoke of dreaming about his own funeral in the East Room of the White House. This so disturbed his wife, Mary Todd Lincoln, that the President quickly dropped the subject.

Actually, Lincoln took a rather calm view about his own safety. "If anyone is willing to give his life for mine," he said, "there is nothing that can prevent it." Lincoln did have an unofficial bodyguard. His friend Ward Lamon appointed himself to the job. Still, there was no official protection for presidents. While the Secret Service was established in 1865, it was not charged with that duty until 1901. By modern standards, the atmosphere in and around the White House was astonishingly casual. It had long been the custom for people just to wander in off the street, perhaps seeking a favor from the president, or just looking around. The halls were often crowded with strangers seeking jobs. However, with the coming of war, four members of the Washington police force were assigned to Lincoln in round-the-clock shifts.

Until Lincoln's death, no one gave violence in the White House too much of a thought. All 15 presidents before Lincoln had died of natural causes. True, someone had taken a shot at Andrew Jackson, but the gun had misfired. William Henry Harrison had died in office—the first president to do so—of pneumonia, and Zachary Taylor died of a severe stomach upset. But, all in all, the White House did not seem too dangerous a place to be.

John Wilkes Booth

Yet, this was wartime, and war makes profound changes in the minds of people. John Wilkes Booth was a strange case in point. Born in Maryland, he was the ninth of ten children in the family of Junius Brutus Booth and Mary Ann Holmes. Like his father and older brothers Junius Brutus, Jr., and Edwin, Booth was an actor. By the time he had grown into a handsome, dark-haired young man, he was a darling of American theatergoers.

Booth grew up considering himself a true Southerner, although he was never apparently motivated enough to enlist in the army. He was a strong supporter of slavery, about which he disagreed with his brother Edwin. He thought Lincoln was a tyrant bent on wrecking the Southern way of life. Devising one wild scheme after another,

Booth fantasized that he would become a hero to the defeated Confederacy. First, he decided to kidnap Lincoln and take him to Richmond in exchange for prisoners. Then, his plans got more elaborate until he devised a scheme to kill the President, along with General Grant, Vice President Andrew Johnson, and Secretary of State William Henry Seward. He enlisted the aid of a number of incompetents in his mad scheme. Their attempts to kill Grant and Johnson misfired, but Seward narrowly missed death when one of Booth's men slashed him with a knife. Never did Booth see that to carry out his plan would do the South far more harm than losing the war.

On April 14, 1865, two days before Easter, President and Mrs. Lincoln attended an evening performance at Ford's Theatre. With them was an engaged couple, Major Henry Reed Rathbone and Clara Harris, daughter of a New York senator. The play was *Our American Cousin*, and the presidential box was appropriately draped with American flags.

Lincoln's bodyguard that night was John Parker. After ushering the presidential party into the box, Parker was not seen again until the following morning. It is not known why he left. Did

A poster at Ford's Theatre in Washington announces the presence of President Lincoln at the last performance of Our American Cousin.

17

"I FAILED."

Major Henry R. Rathbone, 28, and Clara H. Harris, 20, were the presidential guests on the night of the assassination. Married in 1867, their future was forever marred by the tragedy. Rathbone could never forgive himself for failing to protect Lincoln. It is possible his guilt ultimately drove him insane. He murdered his wife in 1894 and spent the rest of his life in an asylum.

the President dismiss him? Lincoln sometimes did that. Was Parker told just to escort the President to the box and then leave? At any rate, Lincoln was left unguarded.

At a little after 10 p.m., after a few drinks at a bar, John Wilkes Booth slipped into Ford's Theatre and walked upstairs to the dress circle. With the audience laughing at a funny line in the play, he stepped into the President's box and fired a single shot. It hit Lincoln behind the left ear and ripped into his brain. The President slumped in his chair. Rathbone turned and lunged at Booth, who slashed his arm with a knife. Then, Booth leaped to the top of the box

An artist's version of the assassination of the President by John Wilkes Booth as Lincoln's wife and friends look on in horror.

DRESSED FOR THE THEATER

Abraham Lincoln was a quiet man, in manner and in clothes. On the night of April 14, he wore a black suit with a long frock coat, a white shirt, a small black bow tie, a beaver hat, and black leather boots, size 14, topped with maroon goatskin. He carried an ebony cane and white leather gloves, which he disliked but wore to please his wife. Although in the turmoil that followed the shooting, Lincoln's possessions were scattered about the theater, eventually everything was returned to the family. These included what the President carried in his pockets: two pairs of eyeglasses and a polishing cloth; a wallet that contained a $5 Confederate bill, probably a memento; a white linen handkerchief with "A. Lincoln" embroidered in red; a pocketknife with an ivory handle; and one shirt button with a gold initial "L"—all on display in the Library of Congress, Washington, D.C.

President Lincoln in his usual neat and conservative black outfit.

rail and jumped toward the stage, shouting "Sic semper tyrannis!" ("Thus always to tyrants," which is the state motto of Virginia). He was wearing spurs on his boots. One of them caught in the flag at the side of the box. Landing off balance, Booth broke his leg and hobbled away in front of a stunned audience and escaped.

The first doctor to reach the President was a 23-year-old surgeon named Charles A. Leale. He was just six weeks out of medical school. When he found the head wound, he removed a clot and relieved pressure on the President's brain. Although Lincoln was breathing, Leale believed the wound was mortal.

The President was carried from the theater across the street to a lodging house owned by tailor William Petersen. Lincoln was laid diagonally on a bed in one of the rooms. His six-feet-four-inch body would not fit a regular bed frame.

A grieving Mary Todd Lincoln kneels by her husband's deathbed. The artist, using his imagination, has surrounded the dying President with various officials and Cabinet members.

As many as 16 doctors visited the dying President that long night. There was nothing to be done, and Lincoln never regained consciousness. Mary Lincoln last saw her husband at about 3 a.m., when she became hysterical and was barred from the room.

Abraham Lincoln was a strong man and lasted some nine hours after being fatally wounded. At 7:22 a.m., April 15, 1865, he died.

Secretary of War Edwin Stanton was one of those at his bedside. Stanton is said to have remarked, "Now he belongs to the ages."

In the North, people who had been holding parties in the streets to celebrate the war's end were stunned and plunged into grief. Equally stunned were those in the South. Hundreds of thousands of African Americans went into deep mourning. And while white Southerners perhaps did not mourn Lincoln and surely did not love him, many may have understood the loss. Certainly with Lincoln died the last, best hope of a lenient, generous federal policy toward the South. What now?

On April 19, 1865, funeral services were held in the East Room of the White House, just as in the President's dream. Mrs. Lincoln and their son Tad were too overcome with grief to attend. Only son Robert, 21, was present of the immediate family. General Grant stood alone at the head of the casket. After the funeral, Lincoln's body, in a hearse drawn by six gray horses, was escorted to the Capitol building. Some 40,000 mourners followed the sad procession. All of Washington was draped in black. The nation had never seen such an outpouring of grief.

The following day, after the public had steadily filed by the flag-draped coffin, a special train began its sorrowful journey to Springfield, Illinois. Along with the President's body went the remains of Willie Lincoln, who had died three years earlier at the age of 12. Each city through which the train passed held its own tribute to the fallen leader.

OH CAPTAIN! MY CAPTAIN!

Millions of mourners viewed the funeral train as it made its 1,700-mile journey to Springfield, Illinois. Poet Walt Whitman captured their sorrow with these words:

Oh Captain! my Captain!
  our fearful trip is done,
The ship has weather'd every rack,
  the prize we sought is won,
The port is near, the bells I hear,
  the people all exulting,
While follow eyes the steady keel,
  the vessel grim and daring;
But O heart! heart! heart!
O the bleeding drops of red,
Where on the deck my Captain lies,
Fallen cold and dead.

A Nation Says Goodbye

In New York City, Lincoln's funeral procession moved slowly up Broadway on April 25, 1865. It was accompanied by 11,000 men in uniform and 75,000 civilians. The procession from City Hall to the railroad station took nearly four hours and was viewed by more than a million people. They sat on rooftops and climbed trees for a last view of the fallen President. "New York never before saw such a day," said one observer.

Chicago honored Lincoln with an escort that included 36 schoolgirls dressed in white, one for each state in the reunited nation.

In Springfield, where Lincoln was buried, the town fathers ordered the statehouse to be covered with black cloth. But not enough was available, so white was used instead. Some people thought that was in bad taste, protesting that white was "too cheery."

U.S. flags fly from black-draped buildings, and mourning crowds line the street as Lincoln's funeral procession moves up Broadway in New York City.

President Abraham Lincoln was buried on May 4, 1865, near his Springfield home. From the day he was shot until the burial, more than seven million people had shared in saying their sad goodbyes. One person remarked, "It seemed as if the whole world had lost a dear, personal friend."

While much of the nation was mourning and burying its beloved leader, where was the assassin? What happened to John Wilkes Booth after he fatally shot the President of the United States and escaped?

There was no doubt who had shot Lincoln. Numerous people in the cast and audience recognized the well-known and popular actor. As the President was carried across the street, Secretary of War Edwin McMasters Stanton took charge. He had guided the War Department since 1862 and was a trusted Lincoln aide. With the President unconscious and Vice President Andrew Johnson at his bedside, Stanton became, according to one observer, "president, secretary of war, secretary of state, commander in chief, comforter, and dictator." At such a time and in some dire situations, such decisive action is usually what is needed.

Stanton immediately issued orders to close the theater, put troops on alert, stop all passenger trains leaving the city, and place guards outside the homes of all Cabinet officers. By that time, however, Booth had already escaped—with the unwitting help of one Sergeant Silas T. Cobb, who was guarding the Navy Yard Bridge in southeast Washington.

On April 20, 1865, a War Department poster offered rewards for the capture of Booth, John Surratt, and David Herold. Five days later, Booth was killed by federal soldiers.

Portraits of accused conspirators in Lincoln's assassination. Booth is shown at top left.

At nearly 11:00 p.m., Cobb, from his sentry post, stopped a fast-riding horseman and asked his identity. Booth gave his proper name. He even volunteered his intended destination—southern Maryland—and explained that he had been in the city late on an errand and was anxious to return home. Cobb, unaware of the assassination at that point, let him pass. Since the surrender at Appomattox, security had become somewhat relaxed in the nation's capital.

Booth was soon joined by co-conspirator David Herold, a druggist's clerk. The two men rode southeast toward Bryantown, Maryland, and the home of Dr. Samuel Mudd, whom Booth knew. Booth badly needed medical attention for his increasingly painful broken leg.

Booth and Herold reached the doctor at about 4 a.m. Mudd set the broken leg, claiming at his later trial that he did not recognize Booth. Much later, he changed his story, saying that he did recognize the actor but did not know he was on the run. It was not until the next day, however, that Mudd, according to his testimony, learned of Lincoln's death and ordered Booth and Herold out of his home.

Back in Washington, good police work uncovered the names of others who were part of the assassination plot. By late April, Booth and Herold had made their way to the farm of Richard Garrett, south of Port Royal, Virginia. After the largest manhunt in American history to that time, federal authorities found them hiding in Garrett's barn on April 25. Surrounded, Herold gave up, protesting his innocence. Booth refused to leave the barn, so federal troops set fire to it. Gun in hand, Booth dropped his crutches and moved toward the barn door. Sergeant Boston Corbett, fearing the assassin was about to fire, dropped him with one shot. On the morning of April 26, Abraham Lincoln's killer died of a bullet wound through his neck. His last words were "Useless, useless."

Secretary Stanton had wanted Booth to be captured alive, but at least the ordeal was over. At the autopsy, the body was identified by Booth's dentist and doctor, who recognized a scar on the back of his neck. Otherwise, the filthy, thin, and bearded actor looked little like the person who liked to be called "America's handsomest man." After the autopsy, a young woman managed to snip a lock of Booth's hair. Police relieved her of the souvenir, but Stanton realized that Southern sympathizers might try to steal more souvenirs. Accordingly, he ordered the body to be buried at a former federal prison called the Old Penitentiary. At night, soldiers laid Booth in a shallow grave covered with bricks.

With Booth gone, a trial for the remaining conspirators began on May 9, five days after Lincoln's burial. It was also held in the Old Penitentiary. Of those implicated in the plot to kill the President, Herold, George Atzerodt, a German-born painter who spoke very little English, and Lewis Powell, alias Paine, a Confederate veteran who claimed loyalty to the Union, were sentenced to death by hanging. So was Mary Surratt. She ran a

HEAR THEIR NAMES NO MORE

After the hanging deaths of Herold, Atzerodt, Paine, and Mary Surratt, a Northern newspaper wrote: "We wish to hear their names no more, and to be permitted to think of our dead President only as a great and good man and patriot gone to his rest, without associating his name with the names of the wretches who have paid the penalty of their crimes with their worthless lives."

boardinghouse in Washington where her son John, who was deeply involved in the conspiracy, often entertained Booth. All four died on July 7. Surratt was the first woman the federal government ever put to death by hanging.

Just before his death, Paine told his guards that Mary Surratt was innocent. But her son John, who perhaps could have saved her, escaped to Canada, then to Italy and Egypt. He was captured and

Having been accused of conspiring to kill Lincoln, tried by a military commission, and sentenced to death, four men and one woman were hanged on July 7, 1865, in the Arsenal grounds of the Old Penitentiary Building in Washington.

returned to Washington for trial in June 1867. Oddly, Surratt was acquitted and lived in Maryland until his death at the age of 72. He never explained why he did not defend his mother.

Conspirators Samuel Arnold and Michael O'Laughlin got life imprisonment and Edman Spangler was sentenced to six years. The longest trial was that of Dr. Samuel Mudd. It hinged on whether the doctor had or had not recognized Booth when he set his leg. By one vote, Mudd escaped death and was sentenced to life imprisonment. Along with Arnold, O'Laughlin, and Spangler, he was sent to the Dry Tortugas, tiny, desolate islands off the Florida coast. During a yellow fever epidemic the following year, Mudd treated both guards and prisoners. The fever killed O'Laughlin, but Mudd, Arnold, and Spangler were released from prison.

Lincoln, the great and good President, was dead, his assassin and conspirators punished. Now, led by a man of lesser talents and smaller convictions, the nation turned its attention to a new policy, indeed, a new way of life. At its best, it might have healed, unified, and rebuilt. It was called Reconstruction, and it did none of those things.

Figures representing the artillery, cavalry, infantry, and navy surround the central column of Lincoln's tomb at Oak Ridge Cemetery in Springfield, Illinois.

RECONSTRUCTION ON TRIAL

2

President Abraham Lincoln, mortally wounded by an assassin's bullet, died at 7:22 on the morning of April 15, 1865. Amid the confusion and panic that gripped the city, a solemn, serious, and impressive ceremony took place at the Kirkwood Hotel. The U.S. Constitution was quietly at work. At 11:00 a.m., Andrew Johnson took the oath of office, administered in his hotel room by Chief Justice Salmon P. Chase. Johnson was now the seventeenth President of the United States. As the Founding Fathers had planned, the transfer of government was orderly and never in doubt. It was, and is, an impressive lesson in the workings of democratic government.

Long before the surrender at Appomattox, Lincoln had been planning for an orderly rebuilding—or reconstruction—of the Union. There was so much to be done. Because the President genuinely wanted harmony to be restored, because he truly wished for a speedy recovery and a just peace, his plans for reconstruction were lenient.

As early as December 1863, Lincoln had issued his Proclamation of Amnesty and Reconstruction, which became known as the "10 percent plan." It said that after pledging loyalty to the Union and taking an oath to obey all laws abolishing slavery, the citizens of any former Confederate state would be given back their property—excluding slaves, of course. After 10 percent of a state's voting citizens—which meant at the time only white men—took such an oath, that state could elect a new government, write a new constitution, and return to the Union. Exceptions to this amnesty included high-ranking civil and military officers of the former Confederacy. By offering the low figure of 10 percent, Lincoln hoped to lure all the former Confederate states back into the Union in quick order.

Many people felt that the plan was lenient and fair, but an important group in Lincoln's own party wanted no part of it. The so-called Radical Republicans, led by Thaddeus Stevens of Pennsylvania, spoke in a loud voice and carried a good deal of weight. They were fiercely dedicated to protecting the newly freed slaves. Rather than a policy of leniency, they believed that the South should be punished for the war.

As advocates of racial equality, the Radicals disagreed with Lincoln on four issues. They felt that the Reconstruction plan should be run by the Congress, not the President. Even moderate Republicans agreed

THE U.S. CONSTITUTION AT WORK

In nine different instances and under different circumstances, the U.S. Constitution has provided for the unbroken, swift, and orderly continuation of the nation's government.

1. 1841: William Henry Harrison dies of pneumonia after 32 days in office; John Tyler becomes the tenth U.S. president.

2. 1850: Zachary Taylor succumbs to a stomach upset after 1 year, 127 days in office; Millard Fillmore becomes the thirteenth U.S. president.

3. 1865: Lincoln is assassinated after 4 years, 42 days in office; Andrew Johnson is the seventeenth president.

4. 1881: James Garfield is the second president to be assassinated, after 199 days in office; Chester Arthur is the twenty-first president.

5. 1901: William McKinley is the third president to be assassinated, after 4 years, 194 days in office; Theodore Roosevelt is the twenty-sixth president.

6. 1923: Warren Harding dies, after two years, 151 days in office, of a possible blood clot, although the cause is in doubt; Calvin Coolidge is the thirtieth president.

7. 1945: Franklin D. Roosevelt dies of a cerebral hemorrhage, after 12 years, 39 days in office; Harry Truman is the thirty-third president.

8. 1963: John F. Kennedy is the fourth president to be assassinated, after 3 years, 306 days in office; Lyndon Johnson is the thirty-sixth president.

9. 1974: Richard Nixon is the first president to resign from office, under threat of impeachment; Gerald Ford is the thirty-eighth president.

with that. During the Civil War, the President had been very much in charge, with the Congress rather following his lead. Now, Congress felt it was time for the President to step back. The Radical Republicans believed that the former Confederate states should be treated as conquered lands, not merely states in rebellion. They wanted the large Southern plantations to be carved up into small farms and given to freed blacks or sold to reduce the national debt. Lincoln wanted merely to return them to their prewar owners. The fourth area of disagreement—and this was a major point—was that the Radical Republicans believed that blacks must be given the right to vote and hold property. The Radicals were not entirely unselfish in this regard. If blacks voted in the South, surely most would vote Republican.

Lincoln was not against the vote for blacks. But although he had freed the slaves, he truly doubted that blacks and whites could ever live peacefully together on equal terms.

Six months after Lincoln's Reconstruction plan, in July 1864, the Radical Republicans offered their own. It was called the Wade-Davis bill and was much more severe than Lincoln's. Although it passed both houses of Congress, Lincoln did not sign it, and so it died. This infuriated Congress, putting it at odds with the President.

The rift between Congress and President grew wider, ending, of course, in Lincoln's assassination. But with Andrew Johnson now in the White House, Radical Republicans patted themselves on the back and began to relax. After all, the new President also detested the rich plantation owners of the South and agreed that they should be punished for their "crimes" against the Union. Said Congressman Ben Wade, one of the authors of the Wade-Davis bill, "By the gods, there will be no trouble now in running this government." Think again, Mr. Wade!

As it turned out, the Radical Republicans knew very little about this man who had suddenly become President of the

United States. Johnson was a Southerner, born in Raleigh, North Carolina, in 1808. His hatred of the former slaveholding plantation owners equaled that of the Radicals. But that's just about the only feeling he shared with them. Their hatred of plantation owners was based on their hatred of slavery. Johnson wasted little time on the fate of blacks or on racial equality. His hatred of rich plantation owners was based on the fact that he believed they trampled on the lives of the "poor whites." The fate of black Americans, freed or not, held little concern. Johnson was a champion of the poor, but of the poor white. He was their self-declared spokesman, and those were the people he felt must manage the South.

Eliza McCardle Johnson

Johnson himself had been born in dismal poverty. In fact, of the U.S. presidents up to that time, Johnson was the poorest. He was born in a shack and never went to school. At age 14, he began to work for a local tailor, where he came in contact with books, probably for the first time. Johnson taught himself to read.

After moving to Greeneville, Tennessee, Johnson married Eliza McCardle, a woman determined that her husband would amount to something. And so he did. With her encouragement, he learned to write and to speak well in public. By 1843, he was elected to the House of Representatives from Tennessee, then became the state governor, and finally went to the Senate. A Democrat, he was by no means always faithful to the party line. This independent thinking often

Andrew Johnson, his wife and two children lived for four years in this tiny tailor shop on Main Street in Greeneville, Tennessee.

CHANGING THE DATE AND PLACE

Since 1933, presidential inaugurations have taken place on January 20. Beginning with George Washington, who took the oath in New York City, they have generally been outside affairs. But occasionally they are held inside. For instance, after James Garfield was assassinated in 1881, the inauguration of his vice president, Chester A. Arthur, was held in the Capitol Rotunda almost in secret for fear that another assassination would be attempted. The second inauguration of Ronald Reagan, in 1985, was also held indoors, this time because the temperature was hovering around zero in Washington, D.C., on that January 20th!

Horrified onlookers, including Secretary of State James G. Blaine, watch Charles Guiteau shoot President James Garfield at a railroad station in Washington, D.C.

brought sneers—usually about his background—from fellow members of Congress. But Johnson was proud of having earned his living, he said, "by the sweat of my brow." Besides, as long as he pleased the voters back home, he worried little about pleasing his colleagues.

During the Civil War, Johnson remained loyal to the United States and stayed in the Senate even after Tennessee seceded. In fact, he was the only senator from a seceding state who did not give up his seat when war began. Largely for this loyalty, he was named to the Republican ticket as running mate for Lincoln's second term in

1864. That inauguration day should have been the highlight of his career to date. Instead, it earned him an unfortunate—and undeserved—reputation.

Following the election, Johnson had gone home to Tennessee to work on Reconstruction. Exhausted and ill as inauguration day approached, he asked to be allowed to take the oath of office in Tennessee. Lincoln, however, realized the important symbol of having a Southerner become vice president. He asked Johnson to return to Washington for the ceremony, held on March 4, 1865.

The 1865 ceremony took place in the hot and stuffy Senate chamber. As he waited to be sworn in, Johnson, who was even more exhausted from his recent long trip, felt ill. He requested something to drink. What he got was a sizeable glass of brandy, and then another. By the time he stood to speak, he slurred his words and was no longer making much sense. Although there is no evidence that he ever had a drinking problem, he became known in the newspapers as a drunkard—"Andy the Sot." It was an undeserved reputation he never lived down.

After Lincoln's assassination, Andrew Johnson takes the oath of office as President in this small parlor of his hotel in Washington, D.C.

But Andrew Johnson soon had bigger troubles than brandy. Forty-one days after becoming vice president, an assassin's bullet put him in the White House.

Optimistic about Johnson in general, Radical Republicans were encouraged by his attitude toward Jefferson Davis, president of the defeated Confederacy. Johnson went along with

War Secretary Stanton's early belief—false as it turned out—that Davis was part of the plot to kill Lincoln. After Lee surrendered at Appomattox, Davis refused to accept defeat and fled into the Deep South. Now, Johnson ordered U.S. troops to capture him. On May 10, members of the 4th Michigan Cavalry surprised Davis and his wife near Irwinville, Georgia.

Davis was accused of treason and sent to prison. Although he wanted a trial, he never got one. Johnson realized that a public trial would give Davis a platform from which to claim that Southerners had committed no crime by secession but had merely exercised their constitutional right. Released on bail on May 13, 1867, Davis returned to his estate near Biloxi, Mississippi, where he died in 1889.

Actually, once the Confederate president was captured, Johnson seemed to lose interest in him. A far bigger problem was how to restore the Union. Although the U.S. government had insisted all along that the Southern states had never left the Union because secession was impossible, a way had to be found to enable the country to live in harmony. If not, all the bloodshed of the past four years would surely have been in vain.

In the summer of 1865, when Congress was not in session, President Johnson issued his own plans for Reconstruction. The Radical Republicans were dismayed. "Their man," it turned out, was far more lenient than they had anticipated. Johnson's Reconstruction—which he called Restoration—plans had two major points. One: Virtually any Southerner who took an oath of allegiance to the Union would be granted a pardon along with the return of property. Confederate high-ranking officers, government leaders, and those who claimed more than $20,000 worth of property, however, had to apply directly to the President for pardons. Two: A temporary governor, William W. Holden, was appointed for the state of North Carolina. Later,

Congressman Thaddeus Stevens of Pennsylvania, strong advocate of a harsh Reconstruction policy toward the South.

Johnson appointed such governors for six other Southern states. Each state must ratify the Thirteenth Amendment, which abolished slavery. Then, the governor, along with members of a state convention, would frame a new state constitution. The constitution would specify, among other things, who could vote. However, Johnson's Reconstruction plans said that only white voters who had pledged loyalty to the Union could be members of the state convention. This, of course, guaranteed that the ex-Confederate states would once again be ruled strictly by whites and it also quickly gave back state control to the South.

Not surprisingly, Radical Republicans were furious. Thaddeus Stevens of Pennsylvania wanted to know if there was some way to stop this "insane course." Also not surprisingly, Johnson's proclamation gave many Southerners the idea that they could simply live just as they had before the war. And certainly not surprisingly, not one of the new state constitutions made an effort to give the vote to freedmen. Women, of course, could not yet vote. The new state legislatures barely had time to convene before they rushed new—and harshly discriminatory—laws into existence.

The new laws came to be known as Black Codes. They had but one purpose—to preserve and protect white supremacy. They did an excellent job. If you were black and in Florida, you had no right to own a weapon. You had to get special permission to preach. If you were black and in Mississippi, each

A DEFEATED GENERAL SETS AN EXAMPLE

A war-weary Robert E. Lee realized that as hateful as it might be to ask forgiveness from the U.S. president, he must set an example. So, once again on Traveller, he rode to Richmond, where he learned that he had been indicted for treason! Lee applied for a pardon on the condition that he not be prosecuted. The matter died there, and Lee was neither pardoned nor tried.

January you had to give written proof that you had employment for the coming year. If you left your job before the date on the written contract, any white person could arrest you. If you were black and in Louisiana, you couldn't even live in town unless you worked for a white person. You couldn't be seen on the street after 10 o'clock at night. And pity the black and white couple who decided to marry. They could both go to prison for life.

Naturally, the Black Codes were intended to limit rights of black Americans. But, more to the point, they were intended to limit the ability of black Americans to succeed economically. To deprive a person of a way to make a living is to limit his or her access to independence, political power, education, and psychological growth. Discrimination, prejudice, hatred, and fear, it seemed, were all too clearly alive and well in the aftermath of the American Civil War.

This newfound power of white Southern citizens led to a new aggressiveness. There were many mob attacks on blacks, especially after large numbers of federal troops were returned North in the summer of 1866. The national government became alarmed, and the Joint Committee on Reconstruction began hearings. Then, President Johnson vetoed a bill that would have extended the life of the Freedmen's Bureau, established in 1865. The bureau had been set up to aid blacks by offering grants to establish farms and, in general, to accept some responsibility to aid ex-slaves in making the transition to freedom.

Radical members of Congress especially were outraged at the veto, which at first they were not strong enough to override. They saw Johnson's action as a disregard for the rights of black Americans, and they vowed to gain control of the federal government. The newspapers began hounding the President; an "insolent, drunken brute" was one of their kinder phrases.

Johnson followed that veto with another. This time it was a

civil rights bill that guaranteed citizenship to blacks and stopped discrimination by states based on color or race. Angry members of Congress began calling the President "Sir Veto." But instead of trying diplomacy, Johnson seemed determined to prove his authority. In fact, he unwisely countered with some mudslinging of his own about Republican leadership. This had the effect of uniting Congress in a show of strength. Accordingly, by mid-1866, both the civil rights and the Freedmen's Bureau bills were passed over the President's vetoes.

Why did Andrew Johnson veto these bills? He claimed that the Freedmen's bill was unconstitutional because it limited the rights of white Southerners. His veto of the civil rights bill implied that he was against giving blacks full citizenship, which he was. Somehow, he seems to have decided that full rights for blacks discriminated against whites. The implication of racism

An important goal of the Freedmen's Bureau was to assist voluntary organizations in establishing schools for former slaves of all ages. This Freedmen's class is being held in 1866 at Vicksburg, Mississippi.

was obvious. But most of all, Johnson's problems with Congress erupted because he was determined to carry out what he thought were Lincoln's plans for a "soft peace" for the South. The Radicals were just as determined to revolutionize Southern society. Johnson declared most of the bills passed by the legislature to be unconstitutional. It was not in the nation's best interests, as he saw it, to grant rights to one group at the expense of another. Also, Johnson seems seriously to have misjudged the Congress. In his zeal to fight the Radicals, he overlooked the fact that many moderates also believed that the protection of civil rights was the honorable thing for the nation to do.

The Radicals wanted to make sure that the privileges of the civil rights bill became a permanent part of U.S. law. So they drew up the Fourteenth Amendment to the Constitution. It says that anyone born or naturalized, meaning to go through the process of becoming a citizen, in the United States is a citizen of that nation. This was the first time U.S. citizenship had ever been clearly defined. It also says that no state could deny equal protection or deprive anyone of life, liberty, or property without due process of law.

To present his views on Reconstruction to the American people before the 1866 congressional elections, Johnson traveled by special train through the East and Midwest, making speeches as he went.

One of the biggest problems in the debate over the Fourteenth Amendment concerned representation and voting. While Section 1 of the amendment made all people born in the U.S. citizens without regard to race, gender, religion, national origin, or previous status as a slave, the same section also declared that no state could pass any law which "abridged the privileges and immunities" of U.S. citizens, and that "no person," even non-citizens could be denied "equal protection of the laws." However, these clauses did not affect voting rights. The original U.S. Constitution did not give voting rights to anyone and the Fourteenth Amendment did not change this.

In 1787, and again in 1866 (when Congress wrote the Fourteenth Amendment), the right to vote was entirely in the hands of the states. After the Revolution some states, like South Carolina, limited voting to property-owning white males. Massachusetts allowed any male over 21 to vote, without any economic or racial restrictions. New Jersey allowed women to vote but this was changed early in the nineteenth century.

Voting and politics after the Civil War were also affected by the allocation of representatives in Congress. The Constitution provided for representation on the basis of total population. However, slaves were only counted as three-fifths of free persons. For example, in 1840 there were just over 737,699 people in Massachusetts and 753,419 in North Carolina. While Massachusetts got ten members of Congress, North Carolina only had nine representatives. That is because 245,817 of the people in North Carolina were slaves.

After the Thirteenth Amendment ended slavery, the three-fifths clause was no longer operative. The four million newly freed slaves in the South were now counted fully for purposes of representation in Congress. Ironically, this meant that the losing Confederate states actually gained seats in Congress with the end of slavery. Yet, none of these former slaves could vote.

Congress tried to solve this complicated problem in Section 2 of the Fourteenth Amendment. Congress could have simply declared that no state could prohibit people from voting on account of race or previous condition of servitude. However, in 1866 Congress was not prepared to take such a bold step.

Instead, Section 2 of the Fourteenth Amendment declared that states would lose representation in Congress if they "denied" the vote to any male citizens over the age of 21. This clause was designed to force the South to either give the vote to former slaves or lose representation in Congress. Had it been enforced and blacks not given the right to vote, the South would have had much less representation in Congress than before the Civil War.

When the South did not give blacks the vote, Congress passed

THE WOMEN WERE STILL LEFT OUT

The Fourteenth and the Fifteenth Amendments did not address the right of women to vote. Nor did they prohibit women's suffrage. The states were still free to give women the vote. However, following the Civil War no state legislatures were prepared to offer the vote to women. Some former abolitionists, like Elizabeth Cady Stanton and Susan B. Anthony, opposed both the Fourteenth and the Fifteenth Amendments because they did not guarantee the vote for women. Stanton publicly joined with racist Southern whites to attack the amendments. These women were particularly angered by the clause in the Fourteenth Amendment that mentioned "male inhabitants" and thus implied that the vote for women was unimportant.

Some women, however, read the new amendments in a more positive way. The Fourteenth Amendment made all people born in the nation citizens, including women. Thus, they argued that the "privileges" of a U.S. citizen and the "equal protection of the laws" included the right to vote.

This feminist reading of the Fourteenth Amendment failed when the Supreme Court, in *Minor v. Happersett (1875)* ruled that the right to vote was not a "national" right, but remained within the power of the states to grant or not grant. The Court did not deny that women were equal citizens of the United States. But, the Court declared that the right to vote was not a "privilege and immunity" of a citizen of the United States. It remained entirely in the hands of the states, provided of course, it was not denied on the basis of race.

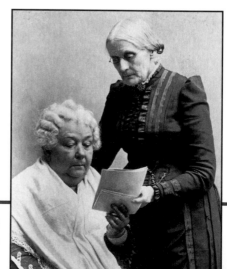

Susan B. Anthony looks over Elizabeth Cady Stanton's shoulder as they work together for their common cause.

and sent on to the states the Fifteenth Amendment, which prohibited racial discrimination in voting. Unfortunately, Congress never fully enforced the Fifteenth Amendment, and by 1900 most of the South had found non-racial ways, such as poll taxes and literacy tests, to prevent blacks from voting. In addition, from 1868 to 1910 white terrorists, such as the Ku Klux Klan used violence to prevent blacks from voting. By 1910 there were almost no black voters left in the South.

Flushed with success, in the spring of 1867, the Radicals in Congress, along with some moderates, pushed into law a series of Reconstruction Acts. They were harsher to the ex-Confederates and went further to ensure the equality of African Americans than anything that had gone before. Freed blacks, white Northerners, known as carpetbaggers, and some white Southerners, known as scalawags, joined forces to take control of the state legislatures. The result was some good legislation, but it was also a period of serious abuse of power and corruption.

Through this unsettled time called Reconstruction, some

Famous American printmakers Currier and Ives combined the portraits of African American members of Congress during Reconstruction. Senator Hiram Revels of MIssissippi is at the extreme left. Included are three Congressmen from South Carolina, one from Alabama, one from Georgia, and one from Florida.

In 1870, Hiram R. Revels takes the oath of office as U.S. senator from Mississippi.

black Americans began to voice their political power. One was Blanche Bruce (1841-1898), a Republican, who was elected to the Senate from Mississippi in 1874. During his term, he fought for just treatment for both blacks and Indians and opposed the existing policies that excluded Chinese immigrants from entering the country. Although Bruce lost his Senate seat when Reconstruction ended, he stayed in Washington and became register of the Treasury from 1881 to 1885 and 1887 to 1898.

Another important figure was Hiram R. Revels (1822-1901), the first black U.S. citizen elected to the U.S. Senate. Born free, he served as a chaplain to a Union black regiment stationed in Mississippi during the war. At war's end, he settled in Natchez, and, in 1870, was elected to the Senate to fill the unexpired term of the former Confederate president, Jefferson Davis. A Republican, he later helped to overturn the carpetbagger government of Mississippi because he believed too many of its politicians were corrupt. Revels and Bruce were the only blacks in the Senate during the Reconstruction period; 16 other blacks served in the House of Representatives.

Considering the efforts of many Southern whites to frighten black voters from the ballot box, it is perhaps remarkable that blacks became part of the voting process at all. Much of the credit for that success goes to the Freedmen's Bureau and also to the Union League. Founded in Philadelphia during the war, the League became powerful in the radical wing of the Republican party. It organized secret lodges to encourage black voters and worked to promote political candidates among former slaves.

After passage of the Reconstruction Acts, over Johnson's vetoes, the breach between President and Congress widened. The House issued an impeachment resolution to determine if the President was guilty of trying "to overthrow, subvert or corrupt the Government of the United States." Stubbornly, Johnson retorted, "Let them impeach and be damned."

Months passed. Despite their zeal, House members were having difficulty finding hard evidence for impeachment. So, the ever-stubborn Johnson came to their aid. In August, he asked Secretary of War Edwin M. Stanton to resign. Johnson was convinced—rightly— that Stanton was on the side of the Radicals and conspiring against him. But Stanton refused to resign. Johnson just ignored the refusal, suspended Stanton, and put General Ulysses S. Grant in his place. Who was going to argue with a war hero?

But, then, January 1868 came around. In this back and forth show of "who's boss," the Senate insisted that Stanton be given back his old job. Grant, perhaps thinking of the presidential election later that year, decided this was a good fight to avoid. He quietly resigned from the office. That seemed to leave a clear path for Stanton. Not so. President Johnson claimed a constitutional right to keep him out and now put Major General Lorenzo Thomas in his place. Stanton retaliated by swearing out a warrant for Thomas's arrest.

There was a sticky point here. The Tenure of Office Act, passed in 1867, barred the removal of a Cabinet member from office

Blacks in the Southern states voted for the first time in 1867. During the Reconstruction period, most blacks voted for Republican candidates.

without the Senate's consent "during the term of the president who had appointed him." (The act was repealed 20 years later.) But Stanton had been appointed by Lincoln, not Johnson. Nonetheless, that was enough for the House to impeach.

The popular notion of impeachment is that it means "removal from office." It does not. Impeachment is actually the same as "accusation," or the legal word "indictment." To be impeached merely means that a public official is formally charged with misconduct in office. Thus, on February 24, 1868, by a vote of 126 to 47, Andrew Johnson became the first American president to be impeached. More than a century later, in 1974, President Richard Nixon avoided probable impeachment by resigning from office. It is likely that Congress would have charged him with misconduct in connection with the Watergate scandal. In 1998, the House voted to impeach President Bill Clinton over charges of perjury (lying under oath) and obstruction of justice.

Only the House of Representatives can impeach. The Senate conducts the actual trial, which is decided by a two-thirds vote and may or may not mean that the president is removed from office.

Johnson was charged with 11 articles of impeachment, the most serious of them accusing the President of violation of the Tenure of Office Act. Article 10 consisted merely of a list of complaints about Johnson's disrespectful remarks on Congress.

The trial began in March 1868. During its three months, Johnson was impatient to the point of agony. He would often pace the White House halls, muttering to himself or to anyone who would listen about the foolishness of it all.

On May 7, the trial ended. Since there were 54 members of the Senate at the time, 36 were needed to convict—a two-thirds majority. Over the next few days, the Radicals learned they had 30 votes for conviction. The President had 12 for acquittal. That left 12 senators—all Republicans—in doubt. Then came the

news that five of the 12 would convict. That left seven in doubt, but the Radicals had 35 votes and needed just one more.

Now, it is May 11, 1868. The Senate reconvenes. The Radicals are in a sweat! They learn that four of the seven undecideds are going to acquit! The Radicals get the vote postponed until May 16. Then, suddenly, one of the four, Senator James Grimes of Iowa, has a stroke. Can he make it for the vote? And what of the three still undecided? Things look grim for the Radicals as they learn that two of the undecideds will acquit. If Grimes can vote, the outcome will be left up to the remaining undecided senator, Edmund Ross of Kansas, a first-year senator, a Radical, and a devoted party man who does not give a hint of his decision.

May 16, 1868, and the Senate is packed. A request is made to postpone the vote for an hour to await Senator Grimes. The postponement is unnecessary as Grimes appears in the chamber, assisted by his colleagues. The vote is now up to Senator Ross. All eyes are on him as he stands and says quietly, "Not guilty."

That was it. Nineteen said not guilty. Thirty-five said guilty. One short of conviction. The impeachment trial was over. Unfortunately for Senator Ross, so was his career. It is not usually healthy to defy your own party.

This ticket admitted one person to the first day of Johnson's impeachment trial. Spectators filled the Senate gallery to overflowing.

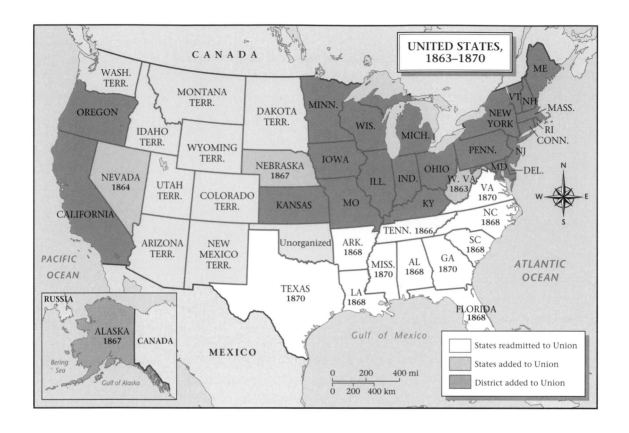

UNITED STATES,
1863–1870

States readmitted to Union
States added to Union
District added to Union

In spite of the Civil War and the troubled times of the Reconstruction period, the United States grew by three states— West Virginia, Nebraska, Nevada, and the huge area of Alaska.

Johnson went back to the White House, Reconstruction, and the business of running the country. But Congress now had control of the federal government and a presidential election was only months away. Despite his problems, Johnson half expected the Democratic party to nominate him. The Democrats praised Johnson for his firm stand against Congress but chose Horatio Seymour, a former governor of New York, instead. Seymour would lose to U.S. Grant in the November election.

In his last message to Congress, Johnson was clear in how he felt about the entire process of Reconstruction. He said, "The attempt to place the white population under the domination of persons of color in the South ... has prevented that cooperation between the two races so essential to the success of industrial enterprise...." In truth, of course, Reconstruction was not an attempt to dominate whites. Blacks never held a majority in Southern legislatures and only once, briefly in Louisiana, did one become a governor. Rather Reconstruction was a turbulent period in American history, a time of hostility and growing hatred.

Andrew Johnson went home to Tennessee still convinced he was right and anxious to prove it. He ran again for the Senate and returned to Washington in 1875. Nervously entering the chamber, he found his desk covered with flowers and heard the applause of his colleagues, even those who had voted against him seven years before. Johnson felt vindicated. That July, at his daughter's home in Carter Station, Tennessee, the 66-year-old ex-president died of a stroke.

In addition to the impeachment trial, another headline event took place during Johnson's term. This was Secretary of State William H. Seward's purchase of Alaska from Russia for $7,200,000. People complained about that, too, at first, calling it Seward's Folly and Johnson's Polar Bear Garden. They thought it was a lot of money for some ice and snow. It still has a lot of ice and snow, but the complaints have stopped. Often called the Last Frontier, Alaska is a vast land of forests, fish, oil, gold and silver, a magnet for tourists, and, since 1959, the forty-ninth state.

THE TROUBLED PRESIDENCY OF U.S. GRANT

3

Ulysses S. Grant may have been the most naive man ever to live in the White House. In charge on the battlefield, he seemed confused by the battle of politics. He had little grasp of economics and even less understanding of the enormous power he now held. This made him an easy mark for self-seeking politicians. He never seems to have understood the potential of his office. In fact, Grant thought that Congress should make all the decisions and he should simply carry them out. Indeed, once in office, Congress treated him like a puppet and virtually ignored his few, mild recommendations.

Nowhere did Grant so strongly show his political ineptness as in the choice of his Cabinet officers. Any hope of inspired leadership died with his first appointments. In the Grant administration, if you were an old pal—or better still, an old war buddy—you qualified for a job. Competence? That was another matter. Grant's secretary of war was an army buddy, General John A. Rawlins. His secretary of the Navy, Adolph E. Borie, had only one noticeable asset; he was rich. However, he resigned in three months because the job took too much of his time. Alexander T. Stewart was rich, too. He was named secretary of the Treasury, but was barred from office because of conflict of interests. The outstanding exception in Grant's Cabinet was the secretary of state. The job first went to Elihu B. Washburne of

Illinois, who served for less than two weeks before resigning. It is said he wanted the job only so he could brag about the title. In his place came Hamilton Fish of New York, competent and steady. He streamlined the department, set up the merit system for promotion, and served Grant well for eight years, sometimes under very trying circumstances.

Grant's White House staff was also filled mainly with old army cronies. This "Kitchen Cabinet" freely gave out jobs to relatives and friends. If competence showed up, it was probably by accident.

A meeting of President Grant and his Cabinet. The President is shown at the head of the table. The most valuable member, Secretary of State Hamilton Fish, is seated at the extreme left.

The results should have surprised no one. Although rigidly honest himself, Grant's administration was soon marked by major scandal, the first to be so shamed. In fact, many historians rank Grant's administration as one of the worst in U.S. history.

Why? Surely, Ulysses S. Grant seemed right for the job. Immensely popular for his leadership in war, he was, at age 46, in vigorous health and the youngest man so far to hold the office. His bravery and loyalty to the United States were unquestioned. When he accepted his party's nomination, he said, "Let us have peace." After four years of Civil War, an assassination, three years of Reconstruction woes, and a presidential impeachment, surely peace was what the nation wanted. And Grant should have been just what the nation needed.

Despite his popularity and promise of peace, Grant was elected in 1868 with only a 306,000 edge in the popular vote. The electoral vote was much larger, 214 to 80 for his opponent, Horatio Seymour. The principal issue, of course, was Reconstruction. The Republicans promised to continue the radical policies that had been passed over Johnson's vetoes. On a lower note, they hinted that there might be insanity in Seymour's family since his father had committed suicide. They also waged what came to be known as the campaign of the "bloody shirt," a term calculated to stir up, especially in Civil War veterans, anger and a revival of sectional hostility, and thus influence their votes. The Republicans tagged the Democrats as the party of secession and treason, an image that lasted for years.

The war hero was hampered by his own personality after he took the oath of office on March 4, 1869. He proved unable or unwilling to consult with more experienced government leaders, who might have averted the scandals of his administration. Also, he showed himself to be totally in awe of rich and influential people. This naiveté brought him all kinds of trouble.

Author Mark Twain called this period of American history "The Gilded Age." His novel of the same name, published in 1873, gives a vivid picture of the nation's capital city. Corrupt politicians and greedy industrialists marked this era of rapid and explosive growth. It was brash, inventive, optimistic, glorious, and shameful. Businessmen demanded land grants or subsidies in the form of financial help from the government to build railroads, protection from foreign competition, and military aid in case Native Americans protested when industry expanded west into their lands. In all other areas, however, industrialists wanted the government to keep out. They found President Grant a willing cooperator.

The scandals that would overshadow anything else about Grant's presidency began during his first term. By the second term, the government fairly seethed with corruption. The word "politician" meant the same as "double-dealer" or "self-server"— a reputation that still hasn't entirely gone away.

The first of the major scandals is known as Black Friday— September 24, 1869. A steep drop in gold prices sent the U.S. financial world into a panic. This was the work of two self-serving speculators, James Fisk and Jay Gould. They wanted to control the country's supply of gold. At the time, the United States conducted its finances according to a gold standard. Money in circulation could be exchanged for actual gold held in government vaults. Fisk and Gould planned to buy all available gold on the money market. With vast amounts of gold under their control, they could drive the prices sky high and then dump the gold back on the market to make big profits.

There was just one flaw in the plan. It wouldn't work unless the U.S. government stayed out of the gold market. If the government decided to sell more of its own gold reserves, the price of gold would, of course, go down. To prevent that action and to corner the gold market, Fisk and Gould hired Abel R. Corbin, the President's own brother-in-law, to use his influence with the White House. Grant seems not to have been aware of this connection. Nor did he seem to realize that by accepting invitations to dine aboard Fisk's expensive yacht, it might look as though the President was encouraging their activities.

Hinting that they had Grant's approval, Fisk and Gould began to buy up gold. In four days the value of gold went from 140 to 163 1/2 per ounce.

A naive President finally saw the light and ordered the Treasury to sell off $4 million in federal gold. The price of gold nosedived and the crisis was over, but not before the market

Famous cartoonist Thomas Nast's version of Black Friday. The street posted as closed for repairs is New York's Wall Street, scene of the financial community's disastrous panic of 1869.

A Dominican Republic Offer

In his memoirs, published in 1886, Grant writes of the incident involving the Dominican Republic: "Santo Domingo was freely offered to us, not only by the administration, but by all the people, almost without price. The island is upon our shores, is very fertile, and is capable of supporting fifteen millions of people. The products of the soil are so valuable that labor in her fields would be so compensated as to enable those who wished to go there to quickly repay the cost of their passage. I took it that the colored people would go there in great numbers, so as to have independent states governed by their own race. They would still be States of the Union, and under the protection of the General Government; but the citizens would be almost wholly colored."

dropped in a panic on Black Friday. Many businesses were ruined, and Grant's administration was forever tainted with scandal. Fisk and Gould were never charged or prosecuted. The United States dropped the gold standard in 1933

Black Friday was followed in 1870 by a scandal more weird than dishonest, perhaps. Grant was informed by Buenaventura Baez, dictator of the Dominican Republic in the Caribbean, that his country was for sale to the United States! The President apparently thought this might be a fine place where free American blacks could relocate. So, he sent his personal aide, Colonel Orville E. Babcock, to talk to Baez. However, he neglected to tell his secretary of state, Hamilton Fish. When Fish got word that Babcock had returned with a treaty, he threated to resign! Fish stayed on, and the Senate refused to ratify the treaty.

As his first term neared an end, Grant was hit with another scandal. This time it involved the New York Custom House. Thomas Murphy was the customs collector, apparently qualified because he used to go to the racetrack with Grant. Just before the 1872 election, it was discovered that Murphy was running a graft system that reaped large illegal profits. With reluctance, the President fired his old friend.

Horace Greeley, editor and publisher of an influential New York newspaper, was Grant's opponent in the 1872 election.

During Grant's second presidential campaign in 1872, his opponent was Horace Greeley of New York. He was the founder of the *New York Tribune*, one of the nation's most powerful daily papers. He was also the man who encouraged people to develop the frontier with his advice to "Go West, young man, and grow up with the country." Greeley's qualifications for president, however, may have been in doubt. Some historians have felt that both candidates for the presidency were not really qualified for the highest office in the land.

Grant won with 286 electoral votes. No votes were counted for Greeley because he died right after the election. The 66 votes he had won were cast for four other Democratic candidates. Grant also carried more than half the popular vote. He was still a national hero. Besides, Americans just didn't think he was personally involved in the scandals.

The next scandal of the Grant administration actually started before his second term. The U.S. government had given large amounts of aid to two companies—the Union Pacific and Central Pacific—to build the nation's first transcontinental railroad. Union Pacific had hired Crédit Mobilier to do the actual building. The railway was completed on May 10, 1869, when the rails from east and west were joined at Promontory, Utah. Three years later, in 1872, it was discovered that Crédit Mobilier was actually owned by the officers, or stockholders, of the Union Pacific itself. And these men were skimming off much of the government money for themselves. Crédit Mobilier got millions of dollars more than the work actually cost, and the officers sold off stock at ridiculously low prices to certain members of the government. The scandal was made worse for Grant by the fact that both his first vice president, Schuyler Colfax, and his second, Henry Wilson, were accused of accepting such stock in illegal deals. So was James Garfield, later the twentieth president of the

United States! Nothing ever came of the charges, however. It was never seriously hinted that President Grant himself was involved, but this was, nevertheless, a sorry spectacle of official corruption and further tarnished his image.

Trouble kept coming. This time it involved the President's secretary of the Treasury, William A. Richardson. He had appointed John D. Sanborn a special agent to collect unpaid taxes. A fine idea, perhaps, except that, in 1874, it was discovered that Sanborn was allowed to keep 50 percent of everything he collected for the government! Richardson resigned.

When the next scandal hit, President Grant was taking no chances. He called for swift punishment. "Let no guilty man escape," he said. This scandal involved the infamous Whiskey Ring, a group of whiskey distillers who defrauded the government by bribing Internal Revenue officials to allow them to pay lower liquor taxes. The fraud was uncovered by Benjamin H. Bristow, secretary of the Treasury. The President may have wanted punishment for the Whiskey Ringers, but not for his private secretary, Babcock, who was also indicted. Although Grant testified to his innocence and Babcock was acquitted, 110 conspirators were convicted.

The last major scandal of the Grant administrations took place in 1876. W.W. Belknap, secretary of war, was accused of taking

An 1875 drawing by well-known cartoonist and political critic Thomas Nast. It shows his approval of Secretary of the Treasury Bristow's prosecution of the "Whiskey Ring."

annual bribes from a trader at an Indian post. He resigned before he could be impeached.

It began to look as though U.S. Grant had little to do in the White House but to recover from scandal after scandal. Indeed, even the integrity and good work of Secretary of State Hamilton Fish—who got the British to pay for damages to the Union inflicted by the British-built *Alabama* during the war—could not erase the incredible spectacle of grafters and dishonest men who ambled through the halls of government during the Grant years.

The President's honesty was never questioned, but the public had had enough. The Democrats won a majority in the House in 1874, the first time since the Civil War. Grant thought about it and then decided he would not run for a third time in 1876. Today, that is no longer an option. The Twenty-second Amendment to the U.S. Constitution (1951) limits a president to two terms.

Grant must surely have become aware of his shortcomings when he delivered his last message to Congress. "It was my fortune, or misfortune," he said, "to be called to the office of Chief Executive without any previous political training .... Under

THE GENERAL REFLECTS

Grant ended his two-volume memoirs with his thoughts on the war's end. "The war has made us a nation of great power and intelligence. We have but little to do to preserve peace, happiness and prosperity at home, and the respect of other nations .... I feel that we are on the eve of a new era, when there is to be great harmony between the Federal and Confederate. I cannot stay to be a living witness to the correctness of this prophecy; but I feel it within me that it is to be so. The universally kind feeling expressed for me at a time when it was supposed that each day would prove my last, seemed to be the beginning of the answer to 'Let us have peace.'"

such circumstances it is but reasonable to suppose that errors of judgment must have occurred ...."

For nearly three years after leaving office, Grant and his wife traveled abroad where they were greeted warmly. It had been his boyhood dream to see the world. He returned in 1879 to find the scandals forgotten and his old popularity intact. In 1880, his name was once more placed in nomination by the Republicans. But this time, they chose James Garfield.

The Grants retired to New York City where a business deal failed and left them penniless. They were saved by the U.S. Congress, who restored Grant to full general's rank and pay, and by a suggestion from author Mark Twain that the war hero write his memoirs.

During the writing of his memoirs, the general knew he was dying of throat and liver cancer. Even after losing his voice and in constant pain, he vowed to finish the job. He did on July 16, 1885, and died seven days later. Entitled *Personal Memoirs*, the book would earn $450,000 for his family.

U.S. and Julia Grant are buried on Riverside Drive in New

Grant at home working on his memoirs shortly before he died. His two-volume Personal Memoirs *was published by the famous American writer Mark Twain.*

York City. Engraved on the war hero's tomb are four words: Let us have peace.

Although Grant's personal integrity was never seriously questioned and his popularity returned, the administration of the nation's eighteenth president is forever marred with scandal. Perhaps that makes it easier to forget that while personal corruption swirled about them, men on both sides of government and the war struggled with the problems of putting the divided house back together. This time the Reconstruction plan was more radical, and that's what it was called.

RECONSTRUCTION TURNS RADICAL

4

Peace did not come easily to the divided house after the Civil War. Many historians call the period—known as Radical Reconstruction—one of the most controversial in American history. For one thing, the balance of power was not in balance. The framers of the U.S. Constitution very much wanted a government that had checks and balances. They did not want a president with the absolute power of a king; nor did they want a Congress that, by sheer numbers, could do as it pleased. That is why a president can veto a bill passed by Congress and why Congress can override a presidential veto if it has the votes—a two-thirds majority. And that is why there is a third branch of the U.S. government—the judiciary, or court, system. The highest court in the land—the Supreme Court—can declare bills passed by both president and Congress to be unconstitutional.

But, in 1869, the checks and balances did not seem to be working so well. Grant, a weak president, sat in the White House. He faced and generally agreed with a strong, for the most part united Congress, controlled by the Radical Republicans and led by several powerful men. Over Johnson's veto, they had passed strong measures for dealing with the South. These measures led to Radical Reconstruction. They were designed to bring equality to all citizens in the area of civil and political rights. Although some Radical Republicans may have been mainly interested in bringing in new voters for their party, others seriously saw these changes as a "golden moment," a chance to bring true equality to the nation.

At first, Radical Reconstruction seemed to work. For all its limitations, it was truly a brand-new idea—an experiment in interracial democracy. In the end, however, it failed and left a bitterness that lingers today. When it ended, with the election of 1876, white power was back in control in the South. There would be few or no advances in the cause of black equality until the civil rights movement and legislation of the mid-twentieth century.

Perhaps the greatest success of the Reconstruction period was the ratification of the Fourteenth and Fifteenth Amendments to the U.S. Constitution. The Fourteenth Amendment (1868) defines citizenship and protects the rights of citizens against state interference. It also provides a penalty for a state that denies the right to vote to any group. The Radicals wanted something more specific about voting, so they introduced the Fifteenth Amendment, ratified in 1870. It said no U.S. citizens could be denied the right to vote because of race, color, or past slavery. The wording did not specifically give blacks the right to vote. It said only that citizens could not be denied the vote because of the color of their skin. This wording allowed some Southern states to deny voting rights to blacks supposedly for other reasons—too poor, too illiterate, or whatever else could be charged as long as it didn't seem to have anything to do with skin color.

The Reconstruction Acts of 1867, passed over Johnson's veto and administered by Grant, declared the existing governments illegal in the former Confederate states. Ten states—Alabama, Arkansas, Florida, Georgia, Louisiana, Mississippi, North Carolina, South Carolina, Texas, and Virginia—were organized into five military districts. A brigadier or major general was placed in charge of each district. The first district, Virginia, was

An 1870 poster showing a parade in Baltimore and a variety of other activities in celebration of the passage of the Fifteenth Amendment.

administered by John M. Schofield; Daniel E. Sickles had charge of the second—North and South Carolina; John Pope headed the third—Georgia, Alabama, and Florida; Edward O.C. Ord took care of the fourth—Mississippi and Arkansas; and Philip H. Sheridan ruled the fifth—Louisiana and Texas. These military commanders were responsible for registering voters, who were to include all black adult males. After voters were registered, new state constitutions were to be written that would guarantee voting rights for African American men.

Tennessee was not given a military government. Unlike the other former Confederate states, Tennessee ratified the Fourteenth Amendment and, therefore, was admitted back into the Union. All states of the former Confederacy had to accept the Fourteenth Amendment, or the Fifteenth if admitted after it was passed, in order to regain statehood.

NAMED FOR A SUITCASE

Carpetbaggers got their name from the inexpensive suitcases, made of carpet material, that many of them carried when they trekked to the South. The fact that a number of them were interested only in their own fortunes gave a poor reputation to all. Milton S. Littlefield, for instance, a former colonel from Illinois, went to North Carolina and made a fortune in state bonds. He became known as the "Prince of Carpetbaggers." But then there was Captain Clinton A. Cilley of New Hampshire. He had been with Sherman in North Carolina and returned to practice law. Years later he won the title of "one of North Carolina's ablest lawyers and finest citizens."

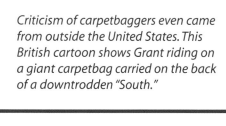

Criticism of carpetbaggers even came from outside the United States. This British cartoon shows Grant riding on a giant carpetbag carried on the back of a downtrodden "South."

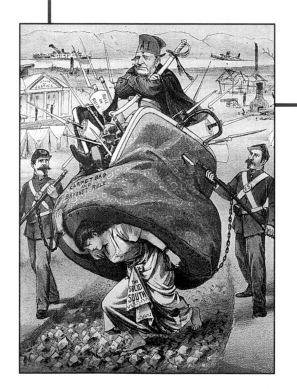

Even if the military commanders were truly dedicated to reconstructing the South in as painless a way as possible, it was a difficult task. It was difficult to maintain order and avoid bloodshed, too. Local Southern officials were generally removed from office. Not surprisingly, the white citizens of the South pretty much detested the military commanders, mainly for their efforts to register black voters.

The Reconstruction Acts are usually criticized for three reasons: (1) The new state governments were run by dishonest whites and uneducated blacks, who, among other things, kept honest Southern whites from voting; (2) these corrupt governments plunged the South into tremendous debt; and (3) all these measures designed to aid black people did just the opposite and, in fact, widened the rift between the races.

Are those charges true? Yes and no. The new Southern state governments did contain many whites, from both North and South, and some were indeed dishonest. Whites who went South during this period were called carpetbaggers, and they earned a bad reputation. They were pictured as immoral scoundrels interested only in lining their own pockets. While many carpetbaggers undoubtedly did go south to plunder, many others truly wanted to help. Clergymen, teachers, lawyers, agents of the Freedmen's Bureau, and even ex-Union soldiers returned to the South to live because they liked the region.

Scalawags were also part of the new state governments. They were about as much respected as the carpetbaggers. Scalawags were mostly Southern whites who had not owned slaves and became Republicans. Some were planters and businessmen. Many were poor hill country farmers who did not want a wealthy slave-owning class in the South. Other white Southerners called them "scaly, scabby runts." One Democrat regarded scalawags as "the vilest renegades of the South, traitors alike to principle and race."

SCALAWAGS FROM SCALLOWAY?

The term "scalawag" may have come from the town of Scalloway in the Shetland Islands, off the coast of Scotland. It was known mostly for the poor quality of its cattle. The term came into use in the United States about the 1840s. At first it indicated a farm animal that was of little or no value. Later, it applied to a so-called worthless person. The term certainly applied to Colonel Franklin J. Moses, Jr., of South Carolina. He had helped to raise the Confederate flag over Fort Sumter in 1861. He quickly joined the Republicans after the war and became governor. Almost as quickly, he began to loot the state treasury.

Some scalawags were Confederate heroes, the most famous being Lieutenant General James A. Longstreet, one of Lee's most trusted officers. Longstreet believed that the Republicans were the only hope for rebuilding the South. Although resented by many Southerners, he moved to New Orleans and became a cotton broker.

*Johnathan
Jasper Wright*

Although it was surely true that many scalawags and carpetbaggers cared not a whit for black freedom or Southern Reconstruction, many did. Some had opposed the war in the first place. Others were just plain practical. They saw the Republicans as their only chance to rebuild the devastated South.

What about the supposedly uneducated blacks who held power in state governments? Only in the Louisiana and South Carolina legislatures were blacks in the majority. The South had no black governors, although Louisiana, Mississippi, and South Carolina did have black lieutenant governors. And one, P.B.S. Punchback, served as acting governor of Louisiana for six weeks. During Reconstruction, several blacks served in Congress, but most of those in government held local state posts. One black man—Jonathan Jasper Wright—made it to the Supreme Court of South Carolina.

The political parties accused each other of intimidating black voters during the 1876 election. In this cartoon, white party workers are "persuading" an African American to vote the Democratic ticket.

All in all, the freed blacks performed just about as well, or just about as badly, as the whites. Some were good, some were honest, some were stupid, some were dedicated. Many were businessmen, often from the North. In general, most of the blacks elected to office were literate and had been farmers, shopkeepers, artisans, teachers, or clergy in Southern towns and cities. Quite a large minority had been slaves.

Did these state governments of carpetbaggers, scalawags, and freed blacks keep Southern white men from voting? Undoubtedly they did in some cases, although the number was probably never large. Many of the Southern states did not even bother to enforce the restrictions against former Confederate voters. In general, blacks in the South seldom were vindictive against whites in their use of newly found political power. They were far more interested in equal civil and political rights than they were in getting revenge. In fact, many Southern blacks didn't even insist on changing the political structure. They were willing to work with whites within the party framework that existed, something most white Democrats were hardly willing to do.

In 1873, the South Carolina legislature in the process of passing a bill providing money for state use.

What about the charge that Reconstruction took the South into tremendous debt? It's certainly true that taxes and state debts rose out of sight in the South after the war. And it's certainly true also that there was corruption. The South Carolina legislature once voted to give one of its members $1,000 after he lost that much betting on the horses! In Louisiana, it had cost taxpayers about $100,000 to run the government for a year. When the Radicals came in, the cost rose to $1 million! Much of it went to rebuild devastated areas. Roads, for example, which had used the forced labor of slaves, now had to be built by hired workers. Of course, much of the money did find its way into the pockets of the legislators. Yet, for all the corruption in the South throughout Reconstruction, there was ample corruption in the North as well—take the Grant administration, for instance.

As for the third criticism, did Reconstruction really help black Americans? Or, did it increase old and breed new hatred and distrust between the races? On that score the answers are probably yes and yes. Reconstruction did not bring about the equality that idealist Radical Republicans had dreamed of. But in addition to passing the Fourteenth and Fifteenth Amendments, they did expand voting rights and modernize state governments. Southern Republicans improved manufacturing and transportation facilities and set aside large sums of money for education. A free school system was created for both races. Before the war, there had been little public education for white children and none for black youngsters. Some 700,000 black children were in schools, segregated to be sure, by the late 1870s.

All this work of the new Southern state governments was done under very trying circumstances. Even though blacks never controlled any of the radical legislatures, they were—for the first time—members of these groups. That fact was enough for white Southern conservatives to denounce these political bodies in the vilest of terms. A newspaper in South Carolina called that state's constitutional convention "the maddest, most infamous revolution in history." In truth, the new delegates were far from mad and not very revolutionary either. They wanted a better political structure, but they had little interest in destroying the old one entirely.

In their search for better government, the new Southern state legislatures weren't helped much by the U.S. Supreme Court. Right from the start, the Court was inclined to be very narrow in interpreting laws passed during the Reconstruction. For instance, in 1875, Congress passed a Civil Rights Act giving blacks and whites equal accommodations in public facilities, except for schools. The Court said no, stating in effect that it was unconstitutional to stop discrimination in public places.

However, even before the advent of Radical Reconstruction, earlier Reconstruction policies, although certainly well intentioned, created more and more serious tensions between the races, largely because of the resentment and fear on the part of whites. In 1866, a terrible fight between black soldiers and white police broke out in Memphis, Tennessee. Over 46 people

A symptom of racial tension almost immediately after the Civil War was this 1866 attack on black soldiers by police in Memphis, Tennessee. Incidents of violent confrontation were to multiply during Radical Reconstruction.

Ku Klux Klan—Hate Mongers

There have been two secret terrorist organizations in America known as the Ku Klux Klan. The first appeared right after the Civil War and the second began in 1915 and continues today. The name apparently comes from the Greek word *kyklos*, which means *circle* and *clan*. Begun, ironically, as a social club for Confederate veterans, it quickly became a vehicle for white supremacy and hatred toward blacks. Dressed in robes and sheets to hide their identity and to frighten blacks, Klansmen staged nighttime raids in which they whipped and killed black Americans and their white supporters. The nineteenth-century Klan reached its membership peak in 1868 and 1869 during which time it was able to keep many African Americans from voting. In 1869, it was officially disbanded by its leader, Bedford Forrest, who also resigned as Grand Wizard, because its behavior had become too outrageous!

However, individual groups continued their operations. In 1870, the federal government began actions against the Klan. More than 3,000 members were indicted, with far fewer convicted. Although the Klan is still a threat today and its members make periodic appearances to demonstrate their rights as U.S. citizens—rights it denies to others—its membership and its influence are reduced.

Terroristic and destructive acts against blacks by the Ku Klux Klan were widespread and rarely denounced by Southern leaders or punished by the police.

were killed and 90 houses burned. Although the tragic incident was initiated by the white police, a city newspaper commented the following day, "Thank heaven the white race are once more rulers of Memphis." Random, senseless acts of violence erupted throughout the South, largely unreported.

But something even more terrible was happening and more disturbing. This was the birth of terror and hate mobs, whose sole function was the intimidation of blacks and, later, other targeted groups. Under names such as the Knights of the White Camellia or the Sons of Midnight, they beat, lynched, raped, and otherwise killed or terrorized blacks and black sympathizers in the South, sometimes for such "crimes" as getting an education. The best known is the Ku Klux Klan, founded in 1865, in Pulaski, Tennessee, with Nathan Bedford Forrest, a former Confederate general, as its leader. As Reconstruction advanced, terrorism became more aggressive and widespread. Cowards who strike in darkness and cover their faces to hide their identity, the Klan has had a long history of mindless violence in the United States. Still today, in periods of civil unrest, the KKK rears its ugly covered head.

Most historians mark the end of Reconstruction as following the election of 1876. The country was in a period of economic decline and marked by constant government scandals. One by one, the Republican governments fell and the South returned to its Democratic leadership.

Besides signaling the end of Reconstruction, 1876 was the year of the nation's most controversial presidential election. The Democrats nominated Governor Samuel J. Tilden of New York. He vowed to end government scandal and to fill political offices only with qualified people. Above all, the Democrats painted their opponents as a party of corruption.

In response, the Republicans called upon Rutherford B. Hayes, three times governor of Ohio. He was a rather bland character but above reproach on the corruption scale.

Late on election night, it looked as though Tilden had won. Even Hayes thought so. Tilden had

Republican candidate Rutherford B. Hayes practices the time-honored political tactic of kissing babies.

To the Friends of
TILDEN AND REFORM!
HONEST SAM. TILDEN,

CAMPAIGN SONG AND CHORUS

BANNER OF
TILDEN & HENDRICKS.
CINCINNATI,
JOHN CHURCH & CO.

TILDEN & HENDRICKS
REFORM MARCH.
CHICAGO,
ROOT & SONS Music Co.

The virtue of honesty is claimed by the Democratic party for their candidate, Samuel J. Tilden, in the 1876 presidential campaign. Tilden had become known as a corruption fighter.

a big lead in popular votes and, more importantly, with 184 electoral votes, he needed just one more to win. Hayes had 166 electoral votes. The vote counts from Florida, Louisiana, and North Carolina were not in, and one electoral vote from Oregon was under challenge. Since Tilden was ahead in Florida and Louisiana, his victory seemed certain.

But the Republicans challenged the returns. They claimed that black voters had been prevented from going to the polls. Indeed, throughout Reconstruction, there were many instances of black Americans being prevented, with violence or scare tactics, from voting.

No one will ever know the true vote count in the disputed states, but the Republican electors claimed victory and sent in their own returns. Not to be outdone, so did the Democratic electors. Now Congress had two sets of returns from each disputed state.

To solve this mess, Congress appointed a commission to decide: seven Republicans, seven Democrats, and one independent Republican. Shortly before the vote, the independent was disqualified and a regular Republican took his place. Not surprisingly, just days before the inauguration, the vote was eight to seven for Hayes.

The Democrats cried foul play, of course, and some modern historians believe that Tilden probably carried at least the state of Florida. If so, he should have won. But it was Rutherford B. Hayes, not Samuel J. Tilden, who became the nineteenth

YES, THERE WAS PROGRESS

The 1870s may have been a turbulent time in American history, but it was productive as well. In 1876, a Centennial Exhibition was held in Philadelphia to celebrate the nation's hundredth year. The upraised right arm and torch of the colossal Statue of Liberty, by French sculptor Frederic Auguste Bartholdi, was erected on the grounds of Fairmount Park. The entire statue would be dedicated in New York Harbor ten years later. Also on display at the celebration were two of Alexander Graham Bell's telephones and a 700-ton steam engine.

Freedom's torch, part of the Statue of Liberty later to be placed in New York Harbor, towers above Philadelphia's Centennial Exhibition.

president of the United States. Tilden had about 250,000 more popular votes, but the electoral vote count read: Hayes, 185; Tilden, 184.

Reconstruction was over. Southern state governments were back in the control of Southern Democrats. What had been accomplished? Did it change anything?

Certainly, most of the civil rights gained by freed blacks during Reconstruction were lost. Slavery may no longer have been legally accepted in the land, but new laws kept the practice of racial segregation firmly in place. Passed by the Democrat-controlled Southern state legislatures, the laws were known as Jim Crow. The name stemmed from an old vaudeville routine—actually, "Jump Jim Crow"—that ridiculed blacks. Jim Crow laws separated whites and blacks on transportation facilities, in schools, parks, theaters, and restaurants.

Once again, the Supreme Court delivered a blow to the fight for racial equality. In 1896, the Court ruled, in the case of *Plessy v. Ferguson*, that separation of the races did not violate the Fourteenth Amendment to the Constitution as long as facilities, in this case transportation, were equal. Thus the Court affirmed the legality of the "separate but equal" concept. Through the

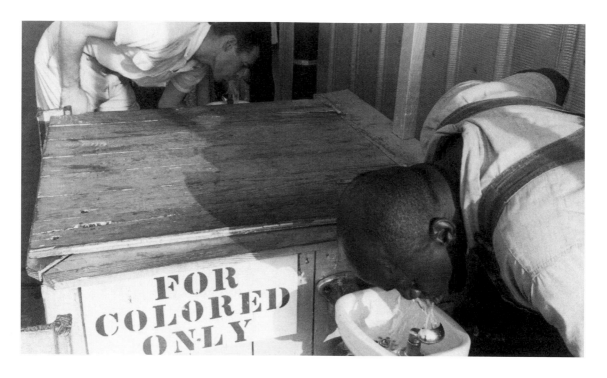

During the Jim Crow period in the South, even drinking fountains were segregated according to the "separate but equal" system.

Through the years, and into the 1950s, additional Court rulings applied this doctrine to education and other areas.

Then came the great change. In the landmark decision of 1954, *Brown v. Board of Education of Topeka*, the Court ruled, by a vote of 9 to 0, that separate was, indeed, not equal and that segregation in the public schools was unconstitutional.

So began the modern social revolution that became the Civil Rights Movement of the 1950s and 1960s. It led to protest marches and sit-ins, riots on college campuses and in the streets, a joining of black and white Americans who decided that the old ways must finally go. During the administration of Lyndon Johnson, Congress passed the most far-reaching civil rights bill since Reconstruction. The 1964 Civil Rights Act banned all discrimination in such areas as schools, voting, work, and public accommodations. Jim Crow was no longer.

Most historians judge the era of Reconstruction to be a failure.

It did not accomplish its aims. It did not bring equality to all Americans. And some of the hate and distrust between races that blossomed during that period continues today. Yet, from Reconstruction came the seeds of change that eventually resulted in the Civil Rights Movement. The pressures of Radical Reconstruction did bring about the Fourteenth and Fifteenth Amendments. The beginnings of an education system did emerge and would continue to grow and flourish. And, however subtly, the Reconstruction era showed many Americans that secession, or war between the states, was no way to settle a fight. The nation was one; it would remain so, whatever the differences, or how difficult their solutions.

In 1965, as part of a protest against efforts to keep black citizens from registering and voting, Martin Luther King, Jr., organized a march from Selma, Alabama, to Montgomery, the state capital. Police broke up the peaceful demonstration with clubs and tear gas. Here King speaks to the angry crowd after the police activity.

FREE AT LAST? WHAT ABOUT THE SLAVES?

5

At the start of the Civil War in 1861, more than four million people were slaves in the United States. In 1865, the war ended and the slaves were free. But what did freedom mean? What could they do with it?

Most of the former slaves had no idea. So few had the education, skills, or experience to cope with the reality of being free. Although they embraced the idea of emancipation, most were not sure what it meant. As slaves, most had been deliberately kept illiterate by their masters. Therefore, the vast majority could not read or write. They did not know how to buy a railroad ticket, purchase goods in a store, or even how to use money. Some had never eaten with a knife and fork. In the end, many former slaves found freedom just too confusing to cope

FREEDOM COSTS MONEY

Many former slaves dreamed of owning their own land. But those who hoped that the federal government would help that dream to come true were doomed to disappointment. "We soon found out that freedom could make folks proud, but it didn't make 'em rich," said an ex-slave. Even a decade after emancipation, only about five percent of the former slaves had enough money to own their own land. Even if they could, they rarely had enough money to develop it.

with. They simply went to work as hired hands on the very plantations where they had labored as the property of a master. It was better to be free, of course, but for many, life just didn't feel very much different.

At first, many of the newly freed slaves just wanted to experience this unknown sense of freedom. Anything that had been denied to them was now to be carried out in excess. Some dressed as they pleased, often copying the fancy finery of their former white masters. Some armed themselves with guns and indulged freely in liquor. Most of all, they hit the roads. One of the most highly resented restrictions of slavery was that no black person could be off the plantation without a pass. After the Civil War, for a while it seemed as though half of all American blacks were traveling somewhere, anywhere just so long as they didn't have to carry a pass.

Tuskegee University, founded in 1881 by Booker T. Washington, a prominent black leader. Washington was particularly interested in training black students in practical crafts. Here students are learning the crafts of carpentry and masonry. The university now offers bachelor's, master's, and doctor's degrees.

In time, of course, this road travel ended with former slaves entering the cities to find schooling and jobs. This dramatic rise in city population flooded the urban labor market and put the former slaves on the lowest employment rungs and in the most menial jobs. Once more they were segregated, this time in squalid shantytowns on the outskirts of cities because that was all they could afford. This influx of blacks into the job market did not please white citizens, especially those who were poor.

An especially sad challenge for freed blacks was the task of finding their loved ones. Auctions had split many black families. They would spend years trying to find each other, and some never did. For years after the war, black newspapers were full of queries from those seeking information about missing loved ones. The search was made more complicated by the lack of records and the fact that, under slavery, most black men and women had only one name, such as John or Maud. When free, many of them simply used the last name of their former masters. This further served to complicate the search for the missing.

In addition, thousands of blacks who had married when they were slaves learned that the government did not consider such unions to be legal, so they had to go through another—and legal— ceremony. Black soldiers who had served in the war were especially concerned that their marriages be legalized so that, in case of their deaths in battle, their families would receive government benefits.

One big change for the freed citizens was the growth of the black religious community. As slaves, it had sometimes been necessary to keep their religious practices secret from their owners. Gatherings for prayers or other services took place at night or hidden in the woods. Now, with the death of slavery came the open flourishing of black churches. By the end of Reconstruction, the vast majority of African Americans openly

A black congregation worships together in this handsome church in Washington, D.C.

attended churches of their own. The church became a great healing ground and place of adjustment to the confusing world in which many black Americans now found themselves.

With so few of the ex-slave population able to read and write, education took on enormous and urgent importance. General Oliver O. Howard, who ran the Freedmen's Bureau, and his staff understood that if people remained ignorant, they would remain, in a sense, enslaved. So, the Freedmen's Bureau organized thousands of schools for black Americans, who flocked eagerly to them. No one was too old to learn.

Right after the war, most of the teachers in the black schools were Northern white missionaries. Not only did they have the task of educating, as quickly as possible, large groups of people of all ages, but they had to endure the criticism and physical threats of white Southerners. If the average white conservative Southerner was against voting rights for blacks, he or she was certainly against teaching them to read and write.

At first, the Freedmen's Bureau bore the cost of these schools, but after 1871, according to the new state constitutions, the states became responsible for both black and white schools. However, the money spent was hardly equal. In Georgia in 1873, for example, black children outnumbered white, but more than $60,000 was spent on white schools and just $3,000 on black.

Not content with the basics of education, the Freedmen's Bureau established about two dozen colleges and universities. At first these were institutions of higher learning in name only. But as time went on, they flourished into respected academic facilities. Among them are Lincoln University in Jefferson City, Missouri, and Fisk University in Nashville, Tennessee, established in 1866 with the contributions and physical labor of ex-slaves and soldiers. Five years after it opened, however, Fisk was in such debt

Fisk University college and Jubilee Hall in about 1873. Once serving black students exclusively, Fisk now accepts qualified men and women of all races.

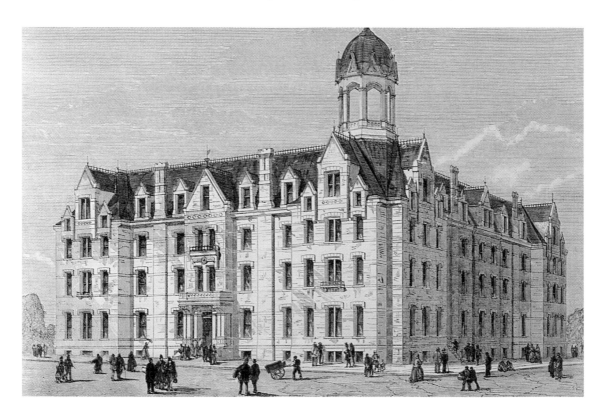

A RECONSTRUCTION HERO

General Oliver O. Howard (1830-1909) of Leeds, Maine, was a West Point graduate and a Civil War hero. A veteran of First Bull Run and Antietam, commander of the Army of the Tennessee, he lost his right arm in the Battle of Fair Oaks. Deeply interested in the welfare of freed blacks, Howard was appointed chief commissioner of the Freedmen's Bureau. Although he was not a gifted administrator and his staff was poorly trained, under his guidance the bureau fed the homeless, built hospitals, provided health care, and obtained work contracts for thousands of ex-slaves. Howard served as the third president (1869-1874) of the university named for him in the nation's capital.

that it seemed doomed to close its doors. Teacher George White decided to take some students and travel north on a music tour. Calling themselves the Jubilee Singers and specializing in spirituals from slave days, the group raised $150,000 and saved the school!

The most famous of all colleges founded by the Freedmen's Bureau is Howard University, named for the bureau's first commissioner and established in 1867. Its first class of teachers graduated in 1870. Today, Howard, made up of 17 schools and colleges, has a student body of some ten thousand students, black and white.

Despite the help of Northern missionary societies and the Freedmen's Bureau, the new black citizen learned a bitter truth. Freedom in no sense meant equality. Equality would be a long time coming, and

Oliver Howard

Born a slave, nine years before the end of the Civil War, Booker T. Washington became the country's most powerful black leader during many of the most oppressive years of Jim Crow racism. His most famous and influential speech was made in 1895 in Atlanta, Georgia.

in some ways it is coming still. Even so, and even with all the hardships of the war and its aftermath, all the bitterness and strife, the end of the American Civil War meant the end of slavery, once and for all time. Perhaps Henry W. Grady, a journalist from Georgia, said it best when he spoke to a New York audience in 1886. Said Grady, "[I am glad that an] omniscient God held the balance of battle in His Almighty hand, that human slavery was swept forever from American soil—the American Union saved from the wreck of war."

THE STRUGGLE GOES ON

Epilogue

The silence must have seemed strange. The guns stopped firing, the cannons on the ships off the coast went silent. Men stopped shooting at each other. It was over.

What happened then? Did the soldiers just pick up and go home? Most did, of course. They went home to lives that would never be quite the same.

At the end of the Civil War, President Andrew Johnson ordered Union troops to stage a grand victory review parade right through the heart of Washington, D.C. With schoolchildren serenading on the sidewalks, about 150,000 troops marched down Pennsylvania Avenue to the cheers of the civilian population. The parade took two days. Major General George G. Meade led his Army of the Potomac in such a spit and polish review that one observer called it the "greatest army that ever went to war." Major General William T. Sherman's men were, to say the least, a contrast. Sherman was never one for spit and polish, and his men reflected that. They looked a bit seedy. Some paraded with dogs and goats and a few carried chickens and hams. Just in case things got too rowdy, however, the officers had removed all ammunition from the guns.

It was a time of relief, but of sadness, too. One soldier remarked that "the rumbling of the [ambulance] wheels seemed like a vast, ghostly procession of the great host of suffering ones who had ridden in them."

I AM THE SOUTH

To Louise Weeks of Hampton, Georgia, born in 1861, her Southern heritage remained forever strong throughout her long life. This is part of the article she wrote two weeks before her death, in 1956, for *The Legionary*, a Sons of Confederate Veterans publication, Columbia, South Carolina: "I was born on April 12, 1861, in the harbor of Charleston, South Carolina, and the Constitution of the Confederate States of America is my birth certificate. The blood lines of the South run through my veins....I am the Mississippi River, the cotton fields of Alabama and the piney woods of the Carolinas.... I am the heritage that is being forgotten, the dying memory of a way of life... Yes, I am the South, and these are the things that I represent. May I always possess the integrity, the courage and the strength to keep my heritage alive, to remain a loyal Southerner and stand tall and proud to the rest of the world. Do not forget who we are; what we are; and where we came from."

A 1995 reenactment of a Confederate charge at Gettysburg. Keeping alive Civil War memories of heroism and misery has been a series of reenactments of important incidents and battles.

Before the year was over, some 800,000 men were mustered out of the Union army. That would eventually leave the new U.S. Army with about 50,000 men.

The American Civil War has been called the nation's greatest crisis. It was certainly four years of suffering and uncertainty. On both sides of the struggle, men fought in such well-known places as Gettysburg, Vicksburg, and Richmond. But they also fought, and died, in forgotten valleys and farmers' fields, in little out-of-the-way hamlets, and near the sides of knee-deep streams.

Incredible as it seems, more than 10,000 battles, large and small, took place during the war. There had been more than a million casualties.

It was indeed a time of great crisis. Even now, so far removed from the mid-nineteenth century, Americans are still fascinated by this terrible fight within one nation, by this terrible struggle that divided our house for so many years.

In many different ways, we are still struggling with and reacting to the problems and the memories of the Civil War. The Sons of Confederate Veterans, for instance, try to keep the memories alive. This is an organization of Southern men, founded in 1897, in Columbia, South Carolina, and dedicated to honoring the sacrifices of the Confederate soldiers and sailors and to preserving Southern culture. An article in their newsletter of April 1997 honored John Caldwell Calhoun, a strong states' rights advocate and supporter of slavery, as a Southern statesman. Another article recalled how Sherman attacked Columbia, ending with the diary of a woman who witnessed the burning of her city; "I would rather endure any poverty than live under Yankee rule ... that word is a synonym for all that is mean, despicable and abhorrent ..." But in another edition, the newsletter praised the contribution of blacks to the Confederate army.

The memory of Gettysburg was kept alive in 1998 with a reenactment of those three days on the battlefield of Gettysburg, Pennsylvania. Men retraced the terrible struggle that ended in a great victory for the North and the beginning of the end for General Robert E. Lee and his armies.

Part of the lasting heritage of the Civil War is the ongoing struggle for equality among all races. The injustices that led to the war and lasted beyond it were behind the confrontations of the 1950s and 1960s and the most important civil rights legislation since Reconstruction.

In December 1955, a quiet black seamstress named Rosa Parks refused to give up her seat in the front of a Montgomery, Alabama, city bus to a white passenger. She was arrested on a charge of disobeying a local segregation law restricting African Americans to the back of the city buses. This event sparked a huge nonviolent protest and

I AM THE NORTH

Here is part of a letter written by Major Sullivan Ballou of Rhode Island to his wife just before the battle of Manassas, or Bull Run, where he died in July 1861.

"... I have no misgivings about or lack of confidence in the cause in which I am engaged, and my courage does not halt or falter. I know how strongly American Civilization now leans on the triumph of the Government, and how great a debt we owe to those who went before us through the blood and sufferings of the Revolution. And I am willing—perfectly willing—to lay down all my joys in this life, to help maintain this government, and to pay that debt...."

The last surviving Union veteran of the Civil War was Albert Woolson, who died in 1956. He was part of the Grand Army of the Republic, which disbanded with his death. Woolson was born in Watertown, New York, and moved to Duluth, Minnesota, where he enlisted. His statue stands in the National Military Park at Gettysburg.

Like the Sons of Confederate Veterans, the North has its own organization, the Sons of Union Veterans, to keep alive the memories of its heroes.

Soldiers in Union uniforms in 1990 representing a Northern infantry unit prepare for a reenactment of the Battle of Gettysburg.

Rosa Parks, heroine and symbol of the Civil Rights Movement.

boycott of the city's bus system, with blacks walking to work or forming carpools.

The boycott was led by the Reverend Martin Luther King, Jr. A federal court finally ruled that this segregation was illegal. After that, King led many protests and marches in support of equality for African Americans.

The Montgomery boycott was followed by sit-ins at segregated lunch counters in such places as Greensboro, North Carolina, when whites and blacks alike demanded the right to sit anywhere. Demonstrations and protest marches took place throughout the South. In Birmingham, Alabama, police chief Bull Connor set dogs on the marchers. And in April 1965, King led a demonstration march from Selma to Montgomery, Alabama. That peaceful march ended in tragedy when a lynch party shot and killed a white Detroit volunteer rights worker, Mrs. Viola Gregg Liuzzo, as she sat in her car. King himself would be assassinated three years later. But the fight would go on.

The end of the Civil War saw the divided house back together. It is unimaginable that it could be divided again. But the scars remain. The North and the South still deal with the problems of bigotry and racism. So, perhaps, it is a good thing that we remain fascinated by the story of the Civil War. Perhaps it is good for Americans to remember what happened so many years past and how close we came to losing the great experiment with democracy that is the United States.

More than 135 years ago, Abraham Lincoln spoke of the house that must not be divided when he gave his Gettysburg Address, November 19, 1863. He ended with these words: "... we here highly resolve that these dead shall not have died in vain—that this nation, under God, shall have a new birth of freedom—and that government of the people, by the people, for the people shall not perish from the earth."

Blacks and whites, men and women, join together in a peaceful demonstration at Selma, Alabama, in 1965, as a somber police officer looks on.

Chronology of Important Events

1863

January 1   President Abraham Lincoln issues Emancipation Proclamation.

November 19   Lincoln delivers Gettysburg Address.

December   Lincoln issues Proclamation of Amnesty and Reconstruction.

1864

July   Congress passes Wade-Davis Bill, which President Andrew Johnson vetoes.

1865

April 9   General Robert E. Lee surrenders to General Ulysses S. Grant at Appomattox Court House, VA.

April 11   Port of Mobile, AL, captured by Union navy.

April 14   Lincoln is shot by John Wilkes Booth; Union flag flies once again over Fort Sumter, SC.

April 15   Lincoln dies; Johnson becomes nation's 17th president.

April 19   Lincoln's funeral is held in the East Room of the White House.

April 26   Booth is captured and killed in Port Royal, VA.

May 4   Lincoln is buried in Springfield, IL.

May 9   Trial of Booth's co-conspirators begins.

May 10   Jefferson Davis is captured near Irwinville, GA.

July 7   Booth's co-conspirators—David Herold, George Atzerodt, Lewis Powell (Paine), and Mary Surratt—are hanged.

December 6   13th Amendment ratified.

1866

March-April   Civil Rights and Freedmen's Bureau bills passed over Johnson's vetoes.

June   Summer Joint Committee on Reconstruction hearings in Congress.

1867

March-March 1868   Reconstruction Acts passed.

1868

February 24   Johnson impeached.

May 26   Impeachment trial ends; Johnson acquitted.

July 9   14th Amendment ratified.

November 3   Grant elected 18th U.S. president.

1869

March 4   Grant inaugurated.

May 10   Union Pacific and Central Pacific railroads unite country at Promontory, UT.

September 24   Black Friday stock market crash.

1870

January-June   Grant administration scandal over Dominican republic offer.

February 3   15th Amendment ratified.

1872

September   Grant administration Crédit Mobilier scandal.

November 5   Grant reelected.

1874

November   Democrats win majority in the House for first time since Civil War.

1875

May   Grant administration scandals involving Sec. Treasury William Richardson and Whiskey Ring

March   Grant administration scandal involving Sec. War William Belknap.

Nov.-December   Rutherford B. Hayes becomes 19th president in disputed election with Samuel J. Tilden.

1877

April   End of Reconstruction.

1880

June   Grant's name placed in nomination for president at Republican convention; Republicans choose James Garfield.

1885

July 23   Grant dies after completing his *Personal Memoirs*.

Facts About Key Personalities

Cited below are some of the key personalities in the post-Civil War period covered by this book. Listed are their main occupations and contributions.

Anthony, Susan B. (1820-1906): Born Rochester, NY. Leader in the fight for women's suffrage. Worked for antislavery society during the Civil War.

Babcock, Orville E. (1835-84): Born Franklin, VT. Served as aide-de-camp to Grant during Civil War. Private secretary (1869-77) to President Grant. Implicated in "Whiskey Ring" scandal during Grant administration; acquitted due to Grant's testimony.

Belknap, William Worth (1829-90): Born Newburgh, NY. Served as brigadier general through the Civil War. Secretary of war in Grant's Cabinet; impeached and resigned.

Booth, John Wilkes (1838-65): Born Bel Air, MD, into acting family: father Junius Brutus, brothers Junius and Edwin. Achieved success in Shakespearean roles. Plotted Lincoln's assassination; killed the president at Ford's Theatre, escaped, was captured and shot (April 26, 1865).

Bruce, Blanche Kelso (1841-98): Born a slave Farmville, VA. Studied at Oberlin College (1866–68). Planter in Mississippi. U.S. senator (1875-81), first African American to serve a full term. U.S. register of Treasury (1881–89, 1895–98).

Chase, Salmon P. (1808-73): Born Cornish, NH. Governor of Ohio (1855–59); U.S. senator (1849–55, 1860); Lincoln's secretary of the Treasury during the Civil War. Chief Justice of the Supreme Court (1864-73); presided over impeachment trial of Andrew Johnson.

Colfax, Schuyler (1823-85): Born New York, NY. Member House of Representatives (1855-69); U.S. vice president (1869-73) under Grant; involved in Crédit Mobilier scandal, ending political career.

Douglass, Frederick (1817?-95). Born Tuckahoe, MD. Name at birth: Frederick Augustus Washington Bailey. Abolitionist, lecturer, and writer. Escaped from slavery (1838), founded and edited abolitionist newspaper, *North Star*. Helped recruit black regiments at outbreak of Civil War. Consultant to Lincoln; U.S. minister to Haiti (1889-91).

Fish, Hamilton (1808-93): Born New York, NY. Member House of Representatives (1843-45); NY governor (1849-50), secretary of state under Grant (1869-77). Negotiated settlement of "Alabama claims" with Great Britain for Civil War destruction.

Fisk, James (1834-72): Born Bennington, VT. Stock market speculator who, with Jay Gould, tried to corner the gold market (Black Friday, September 24, 1869) but failed when President Grant released government gold.

Forrest, Nathan Bedford (1821-77): Born Bedford County, TN. Joined Confederates at outbreak of Civil War. First Imperial Grand Wizard of the infamous Ku Klux Klan; disbanded the Klan in 1869 for "outrageous behavior."

Gould, Jay (Jason) (1836-92): Born Roxbury, NY. Stock market speculator (*see* James Fisk).

Grant, Ulysses S. (1822-85): Eighteenth president of the United States. Born Point Pleasant, OH; West Point (1843). Commanded all U.S. armies in Civil War; received Lee's surrender at Appomattox Court House (April 9, 1865). Elected U.S. president 1868; reelected (1872). Administration marked by scandals. Wrote *Personal Memoirs of U.S. Grant* (2 vols., 1885-86) shortly before his death from cancer.

Hayes, Rutherford B. (1822-93): Nineteenth president of the United States. Born Delaware, OH. Served in Union army through the Civil War. Member House of Representatives (1865–67); governor of Ohio (1868-72, 1876-77). Won presidential election over Tilden (1876), by one electoral vote.

Johnson, Andrew (1808-75): Seventeenth president of the United States. Born Raleigh, NC. Became a tailor, self-educated. Member House of Representatives (1843–53); governor of Tennessee (1853-57); U.S. senator (1857-62). Loyal to Union during Civil War. Elected U.S. vice president (1864); became president upon Lincoln's death (April 1865), served until 1869. First U.S. president to be impeached (1868), but acquitted. U.S. senator again (1875).

Lee, Robert E. (1807-70): Born Stratford, VA. Son of Henry "Light-Horse Harry" Lee. West Point (1829). Led the Army of Northern Virginia through the Civil War. After brilliant victories, was defeated at Gettysburg (July 1-4, 1863); surrendered to Grant at Appomattox Court House (April 9, 1865)—unofficial end of the Civil War. Retired to head Washington College, now Washington and Lee University, Virginia.

Lincoln, Abraham (1809-65): Sixteenth president of the United States; born Hardin County (now Larue), KY. Member House of Representatives (1847–49). Elected president 1860; fought to preserve the Union during the Civil War; freed the slaves of the Confederacy with Emancipation Proclamation (Jan. 1, 1863); delivered famous Gettysburg Address

(Nov. 19, 1863); reelected 1864. Assassinated at Ford's Theatre, Washington, DC, by actor John Wilkes Booth; died April 15, 1865. On any list of greatest U.S. presidents, usually takes top spot, occasionally second only to George Washington.

Mudd, Samuel (1833-83): Born Charles County, MD. Physician and Confederate sympathizer. Set broken leg of Lincoln's assassin, John Wilkes Booth. Sentenced to life imprisonment for aiding his escape. After nursing fellow inmates through yellow fever epidemic off Key West, FL, was pardoned and returned to Maryland.

Rawlins, John Aaron (1831-69): Born Galena, IL. Chief of staff, U.S. army (1865). Secretary of war under Grant (1869).

Revels, Hiram Rhoades (1822-1901): Born Fayetteville, NC. Chaplain for black regiment in Union Army (1864–65). Settled in Natchez, MS. First African American elected to U.S. Senate (1870–71).

Ross, Edmund Gibson (1826-1907): Born Ashland, OH. Newspaper editor; U.S. senator from KS (1866-71). Cast deciding vote for Johnson's acquittal at impeachment proceedings because he believed the trial was unfair; in disgrace with his party, retired from Senate. Appointed territorial governor of New Mexico (1885-89).

Seward, William Henry (1801-72): Born Florida, NY. New York governor (1839-43); U.S. senator (1849-61); secretary of state under Grant (1861-69). Key figure in the purchase of Alaska from Russia (1867).

Seymour, Horatio (1810-86): Born Onondaga County, NY. State governor (1853-55, 1863-65). Made unsuccessful run for president on Democratic ticket, lost to Grant (1868).

Stanton, Edwin McMasters (1814-69): Born Steubenville, OH. U.S. attorney general (1860-61); U.S. secretary of war (1862-68); guided department through Civil War. Credited with remarking at Lincoln's death, "Now he belongs to the ages." Suspended by Johnson (Aug. 1867), restored by the Senate (Jan. 1868), dismissed again by Johnson (Feb. 1868), refused to leave office. Senate supported him and started impeachment proceedings against Johnson. Resigned when impeachment charges failed (1868).

Stanton, Elizabeth Cady (1815-1902): Born Johnstown, NY. Friend and colleague of Susan B. Anthony. Worked for women's suffrage. Led first U.S. women's rights convention, Seneca Falls, NY, July 1848.

Stevens, Thaddeus (1792-1868): Born Danville, VT. U.S. House of Representatives from PA(1849-53, 1859-68). Emerged as leader of Radical Republicans, led move to impeach President Johnson. Died soon after the acquittal.

Surratt, John Harrison, Jr. (1844-1916): Sought for involvement in plot to assassinate Lincoln, escaped to Canada, leaving his mother, Mary, to face hanging. Returned later and was acquitted of involvement (1867).

Surratt, Mary Eugenia (1817-65): Born Waterloo, MD. Operated boardinghouse in Washington, D.C., where Booth supposedly devised plot to assassinate Lincoln. Arrested and tried for participating in the conspiracy; although she protested innocence, was found guilty and hanged (1865).

Tilden, Samuel J. (1814-86): Born New Lebanon, NY. State governor (1875-76). Democratic candidate for president (1876), lost to Rutherford B. Hayes in questionable election. Bequeathed fortune to establish a free public library in New York City.

Wade, Benjamin Franklin (1800-78): Born Springfield, MA. U.S. senator from OH (1851-69). Became a leading radical during Reconstruction, sponsored strict Wade-Davis bill for dealing with the South after Civil War. After veto by Johnson, pursued impeachment proceedings. Had Johnson been convicted, Wade, as president pro tempore of the Senate, would have succeeded him. Wade was so sure of conviction that he had begun to select his Cabinet before trial ended. Retired 1869.

Wilson, Henry (1812-75): Born Jeremiah Jones Colbath, Farmington, NH. Founded Free-Soil party. U.S. senator from MA (1855-73), a founder of Republican party. Strongly opposed Andrew Johnson. U.S. vice president (1873-75) under Grant.

Glossary

abolitionist	One who supports the end of slavery.
acquittal	The act of setting free from a sentence or other legal charge.
advocate	A supporter, one who pleads the cause of another.
aftermath	The period following a usually harmful event, such as the Civil War.
allegiance	Devotion or loyalty to a person or cause.
aristocracy	A grouping of those believed to be superior.
assassin	One who commits murder, especially murder of a politically prominent person.
auction	Sale of property to the highest bidder.
autopsy	An examination after the event, such as a physical exam of a body after death.
Black Codes	Laws adopted by some southern states after the Civil War to limit rights of newly freed black Americans.
bodyguard	A person paid to safeguard the life of another.
bond	An interest-bearing certificate of public or private indebtedness, often used to finance public buildings or works.
boomtown	A town that experiences rapid growth, such as from the discovery of gold nearby.
byways	Little-traveled roads.
conspirator	One who acts in harmony toward a common end; one who joins in secret agreement to accomplish an unlawful act.
contract	Binding agreement between two persons or parties, especially one that is legally enforceable.
cronies	Long-standing old friends, pals.
diplomacy	Practice of conducting negotiations between nations.
dress circle	First or lowest curved tier of seats above main floor in opera house or theater.
due process	Legal proceedings carried out according to established principles and laws of the land.
emancipation	Act or process of freeing from bondage, as slaves.
feminist	One who advocates rights and interests of women.
frontier	Generally, a region marking the border of unsettled lands.

gentry	Upper or ruling class. *See* aristocracy.
graft	Gain (as money) in dishonest ways.
hearse	Special vehicle for conveying the dead to gravesite.
immigrant	A person who comes to a country to live permanently.
impeachment	The act of charging a person, usually a public official, with a crime or misconduct.
infraction	Violation of a law.
land grant	The offer of land by the government, usually for a specific purpose, such as building a railroad.
liberal	In politics, one who favors economic freedom, greater individual participation in government.
literate	Being able to read and write.
manhunt	Organized, intensive search for one suspected of a crime.
memoirs	Narrative of a personal experience.
merit system	Civil service appointments based on competence over political favoritism.
missionary	One who carries out humanitarian work.
mourners	Those who show signs of grief, generally over death of loved ones.
mudslinging	One who uses vile terms, especially against a political opponent.
naturalize	To give the rights of citizenship.
network	Interconnected system of lines or channels.
overseer	Superintendent or supervisor.
pardon	Release from legal penalties of an offense.
plunder	To take by force, especially during a war.
postponement	Act of deferring to a later time.
proclamation	Official, formal public announcement.
racism	A belief that racial differences prove the superiority of a certain race.
radical	One who believes in extreme measures to keep or restore a state of political affairs.
Radical Republican	Member of Congress after Civil War fighting for full equality of blacks.
ratify	To approve formally, such as an amendment to the Constitution.
rebellion	Open, armed defiance of established government.

Glossary

reconstruction	The act of rebuilding, as in rebuilding the nation after the Civil War.
rotunda	Round building, especially one covered by a dome, as the Capitol rotunda in Washington, D.C.
scandal	Supposed conduct that brings disgrace.
scoundrel	A person of disreputable behavior.
secession	Formal withdrawal from an organization, such as the Southern states seceding from the United States.
segregation	Separation or isolation of a certain, usually racial or ethnic, group.
sentry	Soldier standing guard at a specific point, as a gate.
shantytown	Poor village or city section made of crude dwellings.
speculator	One who assumes business risk in hope of gain.
spirituals	Religious songs of deeply emotional character, such as among black Americans in pre-Civil War years.
subsidy	A grant or gift of money, usually for a specific purpose.
suffrage	The right of voting.
symbol	Visible sign of something invisible, such as a lion may stand for courage.
testimony	Statement given by witness under oath.
traitor	One who betrays a trust or is false to one's duty.
treason	Overt act to overthrow one's government.
typhoid fever	Communicable disease marked by fever, headache, and intestinal inflammation.
tyrant	Ruler who exercises absolute power oppressively.
warrant	A document giving the legal authority for a certain action, such as arresting someone.
white supremacy	Belief in the inherent superiority of white over other races.

Bibliography

American Heritage Book of the Presidents, 12 vols. New York: Dell, 1967.

Bradford, Ned. *Battles and Leaders of the Civil War*. New York: Appleton, 1956.

Catton, Bruce. *The American Heritage New History of the Civil War*. New York: Viking, 1996.

Commager, Henry Steele. *The Blue and the Gray*. New York: Bobbs-Merrill, 1950.

_____. *Documents of American History*, 10th ed. Englewood Cliffs, NJ: Prentice-Hall, 1988.

Davis, William C., ed. *The Civil War*. Alexandria, VA: Time-Life Books, 1983, 28 vols.

Encyclopedia Britannica, 15th ed.

Foner, Eric. *A Short History of Reconstruction*. New York: Harper, 1990.

Gruver, Rebecca Brooks. *An American History*, Vol. 1. London: Addison-Wesley, 1972.

Long, E.B. *The Civil War Day by Day: An Almanac 1861-1865*. New York: Doubleday, 1971.

McPherson, James. W. *For Cause & Comrades: Why Men Fought in the Civil War*. New York: Oxford Univ. Press, 1997.

Ward, Geoffrey C. *The Civil War: An Ilustrated History*. New York: Knopf, 1990.

Further Reading

Banfield, Susan. *The Fifteenth Amendment: African-American Men's Right to Vote*. Springfield, NJ: Enslow, 1998.

Collier, C. and Collier, J.L. *The Reconstruction Era, 1864-1877* (Drama of American History series). Tarrytown, NY: Marshall Cavendish, 1999.

Edwards, Cheryl. *Reconstruction: Binding the Wounds* (Perspective on History series). Carlisle, MA: Discovery Enterprises, 1995.

Genovese, Eugen D.A. *A Consuming Fire: The Fall of the Confederacy in the Mind of the White Christian South*. Athens, GA: University of Georgia Press, 1999.

Otfinoski, Steven. *John Wilkes Booth and the Civil War* (Notorious Americans and Their Times series). Woodbridge, CT: Blackbirch, 1998.

Posner, Gerald. *Killing the Dream: James Earl Ray and the Assassination of Martin Luther King, Jr.* New York: Random House, 1998

Rasmussen, R. Kent. *Farewell to Jim Crow: The Rise and Fall of Segregation in America* (Library of African-American History series). New York: Facts on File, 1997.

Schleichert, Elizabeth. *The Thirteenth Amendment: Ending Slavery*. Springfield, NJ: Enslow, 1998.

Smith, John David. *Black Voices from Reconstruction, 1865-1877*. Brookfield, CT: Millbrook, 1996.

Weatherford, Doris. *A History of the American Suffragist Movement*. Santa Barbara, CA: ABC-Clio, 1998.

Werner, Emmy E. *Reluctant Witnesses: Children's Voices from the Civil War*. Boulder, CO: Westview, 1998.

Zeinert, Karen. *The Lincoln Murder Plot*. North Haven, CT: Shoe String/Linnet, 1999.

Websites

Here are a few suggested websites with information relevant to the contents of this book. The authors and the editors take no responsibility for the accuracy of any information found on the Internet. Nor can we guarantee the availability of any website.

The Civil War and Reconstruction (1850 to 1877)
A collection of biographies, documents and army unit information concerned with the Civil War and Reconstruction (1850 to 1877). Includes slave life–families, religion, and resistance in the American South–a nation divided, and the failed attempts at compromise over slavery.
http://quaboag.k12.ma.us/civwar.html

Ford's Theatre–National Historical Site
The national park service website for Ford's Theatre. This site contains a wide variety of topics on the conspiracy and Lincoln's assassination.
http://www.nps.gov/foth/index2.htm

The Freedmen's Bureau - 01.03
This website has information about the early days of the Freedmen's Bureau in the years following the Civil War.
http://www3.theatlantic.com/atlantic/issues/01mar/dubois.htm

The Impeachment of Andrew Johnson
This website covers the impeachment of Andrew Johnson from the viewpoint of the leading weekly newspaper of its time. HarpWeek presents exclusive online access to *Harper's Weekly* coverage of the historic 1868 Johnson impeachment—with over 200 excerpts from 1865–1869—selected specifically for this site.
http://www.impeach-andrewjohnson.com/default.htm

The Life and Times of U.S. Grant, President and General
Information about Grant's early life, his participation in the Civil War, and his first and second administrations (1822-1885).
http://www.solutionassociates.com/grant/bio.htm

Texas and Reconstruction

There are many opportunities to use Texas examples in learning about United States history during the period of Reconstruction. The most obvious ones are the political aspects of Reconstruction common to the other states of the Confederacy.
http://riceinfo.rice.edu/amardillo/Texas/Sharedpast/linkreco...

Timelines of the Reconstruction–List of Sources

Here are a list of sources for information from the Congressional Globe, 37th Congress through 42nd Congress (1861 through 1873), and the Congressional Record, 43rd Congress through 56th Congress (1873 through 1901).
http://www.ameritech.net/users/jklann/SOURCES.HTM

Index

Note: Page numbers in italics indicate illustrations or maps.

Index

Index

Index

Acknowledgments

Cover: CORBIS/Bettmann; p.3 CORBIS/Digital Stock; p.6 CORBIS/Bettmann; p.8 The Granger Collection; p.9 CORBIS/Digital Stock; p.11 CORBIS; p.12 CORBIS/Digital Stock; p.13 Library of Congress; p.14 National Portrait Gallery/Smithsonian Institution; p.15 The Granger Collection; p.16 Culver Pictures, Inc.; p.17 CORBIS/Bettmann; p.18 The Granger Collection; p.19 Corbis/Digital Stock; pp.20, 22 The Granger Collection; p.23 National Archives; p.24 CORBIS; p.26 CORBIS/Digital Stock; p.27 ©Brian Seed/Tony Stone Images; p.30 The Granger Collection; p.31 (t) Library of Congress; p.31 (b) CORBIS; p.32 The Granger Collection; p.33 CORBIS/Bettmann; p.37 State Historical Society of Missouri; pp.38, 40 CORBIS; p.41 The Granger Collection; p.42 CORBIS/Bettmann; p.43 ©North Wind Pictures; pp.45, 49 CORBIS/Bettmann; p.52 The Granger Collection; p.53 CORBIS; p.55 The Granger Collection; p.57 CORBIS/Bettmann; p.58 CORBIS/Robert Holmes; pp.61, 62, 64 (both) The Granger Collection; p.65 ©North Wind Pictures; pp.67, 68 The Granger Collection; pp.69, 70 CORBIS/Bettman; p.71 The Granger Collection; p.72 CORBIS/Bettmann; p.73 UPI Telephoto; p.75 UPI/Corbis-Bettmann; pp.77, 78 ©North Wind Pictures; p.79 The Granger Collection; p.80 CORBIS/Bettmann; pp.82-83, 84-85 CORBIS/Richard T. Nowitz; p.86 United Press International; p.87 CORBIS/Flip Schulke.

Map design & production: Tina Graziano, MapQuest.com